Lecture Notes in Computer Science 16317

Founding Editors

Gerhard Goos
Juris Hartmanis

Editorial Board Members

Elisa Bertino, *Purdue University, West Lafayette, IN, USA*
Wen Gao, *Peking University, Beijing, China*
Bernhard Steffen, *TU Dortmund University, Dortmund, Germany*
Moti Yung, *Columbia University, New York, NY, USA*

The series Lecture Notes in Computer Science (LNCS), including its subseries Lecture Notes in Artificial Intelligence (LNAI) and Lecture Notes in Bioinformatics (LNBI), has established itself as a medium for the publication of new developments in computer science and information technology research, teaching, and education.

LNCS enjoys close cooperation with the computer science R & D community, the series counts many renowned academics among its volume editors and paper authors, and collaborates with prestigious societies. Its mission is to serve this international community by providing an invaluable service, mainly focused on the publication of conference and workshop proceedings and postproceedings. LNCS commenced publication in 1973.

Jieyun Bai · Yuxin Huang · Isaac Khobo ·
Mohammad Yaqub · Karim Lekadir · Dong Ni ·
Shuo Li

Editors

Intrapartum Ultrasound

MICCAI 2025 Grand Challenge, IUGC 2025
Held in Conjunction with MICCAI 2025
Daejeon, South Korea, September 23, 2025
Proceedings

 Springer

Editors
Jieyun Bai
Jinan University
Guangzhou, China

Isaac Khobo
University of Cape Town
Cape Town, South Africa

Karim Lekadir (ID)
Universitat de Barcelona
Barcelona, Spain

Shuo Li
Case Western Reserve University
Cleveland, OH, USA

Yuxin Huang
Southern Medical University
Guangzhou, China

Mohammad Yaqub
Mohamed bin Zayed University of Artificial
Intelligence
Abu Dhabi, United Arab Emirates

Dong Ni
Shenzhen University
Shenzhen, China

ISSN 0302-9743　　　　　ISSN 1611-3349　(electronic)
Lecture Notes in Computer Science
ISBN 978-3-032-11615-4　　　ISBN 978-3-032-11616-1　(eBook)
https://doi.org/10.1007/978-3-032-11616-1

Preface

This volume presents the proceedings of the Intrapartum Ultrasound Grand Challenge 2025 (IUGC 2025) Landmark Detection Challenge for Intrapartum Ultrasound Measurement Meeting the Actual Clinical Assessment of Labor Progress, held in conjunction with the International Conference on Medical Image Computing and Computer-Assisted Interventions (MICCAI) in 2025: The proceedings feature papers submitted by participants that describe their innovative methods for automating landmark detection and biometric measurement of fetal head descent using intrapartum ultrasound imaging, based on the official dataset released for this challenge.

Accurate monitoring of labor progression is central to safe intrapartum care, yet traditional vaginal examinations for assessing fetal station remain highly subjective, invasive, and prone to error rates as high as 34%. In contrast, intrapartum ultrasound has emerged as a reproducible and objective modality for quantifying labor progression through parameters such as the Angle of Progression (AoP). However, the clinical adoption of ultrasound is constrained by operator dependency and the challenge of reliably identifying anatomical landmarks in real time. IUGC 2025 addressed these limitations by advancing artificial intelligence (AI)-driven approaches for fully automatic, end-to-end landmark detection, thereby reducing observer variability and enabling robust, bedside-ready solutions.

Building on prior editions of the challenge, which focused on segmentation-based workflows (PSFHS 2023 and IUGC 2024), IUGC 2025 introduced a paradigm shift toward direct landmark detection. Participants were tasked with detecting three anatomical landmarks—two points on the pubic symphysis and one on the fetal skull—from intrapartum ultrasound standard planes and computing the AoP. This design leverages semi-supervised learning to combine a limited number of labeled cases with a large pool of unlabeled data, aiming to overcome the bottleneck of costly annotations while improving model generalizability. The dataset comprised 32,022 images from 24 institutions worldwide, including 300 expertly annotated cases, 31,121 unlabeled cases, 100 validation cases, and 501 held-out test cases, collected using diverse ultrasound systems. Evaluation was based on both geometric accuracy—measured by Mean Radial Error (MRE)—and clinical agreement, assessed via the absolute error in AoP estimation relative to manual reference measurements.

The challenge attracted 81 registered teams, with 53 actively participating and 27 submissions received before the deadline. Eleven papers were accepted after a single-blind review process in which submissions received on average two reviews each. These eleven teams presented their methods at the associated workshop, the 6th International Workshop on Advances in Simplifying Medical UltraSound (ASMUS 2025). Top-performing solutions explored semi-supervised frameworks, self-supervised pretraining, transformer-based backbones, adversarial learning, and pseudo-labeling strategies, highlighting the growing diversity and sophistication of AI approaches in intrapartum imaging.

Compared with previous editions, IUGC 2025 emphasized clinical applicability by focusing on end-to-end biometric measurement directly from landmarks, covering all fetal head descent stations, and benchmarking methods against both algorithmic performance and inter-observer variability. By releasing the dataset, annotations, evaluation scripts, and accepted papers, IUGC 2025 provides the first fully open benchmark for landmark detection in intrapartum ultrasound, thereby establishing a foundation for future innovation and translation into clinical practice.

We extend our gratitude to all participants, reviewers, and the organizing committee, including clinicians and AI researchers worldwide, for their commitment to advancing maternal and neonatal health through technology. Special thanks are due to Guangzhou Lian-Med Technologies Co., Ltd. for their sponsorship and data support. This study was supported by project grants from the Natural Science Foundation of Guangdong Province (2024A1515011886), the National Institute of Hospital Administration (No. YLXX24AIA006), Sichuan Provincial Cross-Regional Innovation Cooperation Project (No. 2025YFHZ0326), and Key Research and Development Program of Guangxi Province (No. 2023AB22074 and 2024AB04027), the National Natural Science Foundation of China (61901192), the Guangzhou Science and Technology Planning Project (2023B03J1297), the Guangzhou Municipal Science and Technology Bureau Guangzhou Key Research and Development Program (2024B03J1283 and 2024B03J1289), the High-end Foreign Experts Recruitment Plan of China (H20240205), the China Scholarship Council (202206785002), and the European Research Council (ERC) under the Horizon Europe programme (AIMIX project – Grant Agreement No. 101044779).

September 2025

Jieyun Bai
Yuxing Huang
Yaosheng Lu
Mohammad Yaqub
Karim Lekadir
Dong Ni
Shuo Li

Organization

Organizing Committee

Jieyun Bai	Jinan University, China
Yitong Tang	Jinan University, China
Zihao Zhou	Jinan University, China

Program Committee

Karim Lekadir	University of Barcelona, Spain
Dong Ni	Shenzhen University, China
Saad Slimani	Ibn Rochd University Hospital, Hassan II University, Morocco
Ziduo Yang	Jinan University, China
Mohamed Hammad	Prince Sultan University, Saudi Arabia
Yaosheng Lu	Jinan University, China
Yuxing Huang	Zhujiang Hospital of Southern Medical University, China
Hongying Hou	Third Affiliated Hospital of Sun Yat-sen University, China
XiaoMeng Li	Hong Kong University of Science and Technology, China
Di Qiu	First Affiliated Hospital of Jinan University, China
Mohammad Yaqub	Mohamed bin Zayed University of Artificial Intelligence, United Arab Emirates
Zheng Zheng	Guangzhou Women and Children's Medical Center, Guangzhou Medical University, China
Isaac Khobo	University of Cape Town, South Africa
Jun Ma	University of Toronto, Canada
Shuo Li	Case Western Reserve University, USA

Contents

Noisy Student-Based Self-training Enhances Landmark Detection in Intrapartum Ultrasound

Xiao Liu[1], Jiale Hu[1]($\boxtimes$), Yunda Li[1], Xufan Chen[1], and Yufeng Wang[2]

[1] School of Computer and Software, Nanyang Institute of Technology,
Nanyang 473004, China
`2215925709@nyist.edu.cn`

[2] Academy for Electronic Information Discipline Studies, Nanyang Institute of
Technology, Nanyang 473004, China

Abstract. Accurate detection of fetal anatomical landmarks in ultrasound images during labor is crucial for clinical labor assessment. Despite significant progress in deep learning for medical image analysis, achieving high-precision and robust keypoint detection remains challenging under the realistic condition of scarce annotated data. Inspired by the Noisy Student paradigm in image classification, this paper proposes an improved semi-supervised method tailored for keypoint detection tasks. We construct a DenseUNet teacher-student framework to perform collaborative training using limited annotated data and a portion of unlabeled images. Specifically, the teacher model is trained on the labeled set to generate heatmap pseudo-labels for the unlabeled data; the student model, supervised by the pseudo-labels, leverages the dense connectivity of DenseNet to enhance feature reuse and gradient flow, and incorporates Dropout in the decoder to improve robustness. Furthermore, a linearly-decayed MixUp strategy is adopted for input perturbation, combined with heatmap supervision, to achieve a smooth transition from strong perturbation training to stable convergence. Experiments on the IUGC 2025 test set demonstrate that the proposed method significantly improves landmark detection performance, achieving an average distance error (Distance) of 13.1574 and an AOP_MAE score of 4.4244, which verifies the effectiveness of the method in scenarios with limited annotation resources. The project source code is available at: https://github.com/apuomline/IUGC2025.

Keywords: Anatomical landmark detection · Intrapartum ultrasound · Semi-supervised learning · Noisy Student framework

1 Introduction

Accurate assessment of fetal head descent during labor is crucial for reducing the risks of dystocia and cesarean delivery. According to the World Health Organization's 2020 Guidelines on Intrapartum Care for a Positive Birth Experience,

J. Bai et al. (Eds.): IUGC 2025, LNCS 16317, pp. 1–13, 2026.
https://doi.org/10.1007/978-3-032-11616-1_1

real-time monitoring of fetal head progression is one of the core intervention measures. Among these, the Angle of Progression (AoP) serves as a key indicator for quantifying this process. It is formed by two points at the distal end of the pubic symphysis and one point on the fetal head. However, the current measurement of AoP still relies on experienced clinicians to manually annotate each frame, which is time-consuming and subject to significant inter-observer variability.

To address the aforementioned limitations, the MICCAI 2025 Intrapartum Ultrasound Challenge (IUGC 2025) introduced [1] a semi-supervised end-to-end keypoint detection method for AoP estimation. Unlike the standard two-stage approach of segmentation [2] followed by measurement, this approach directly regresses the coordinates of the three anatomical landmarks from transperineal ultrasound images and outputs the AoP in real time, enabling zero-interaction and fully automatic measurement. This dataset covers nine descent stations of fetal head presentation ranging from -5 to $+3$ and includes 32,000 multicenter images, making it the largest and most comprehensive intrapartum ultrasound image repository to date. The 501 hidden test samples were independently annotated by multiple experts, ensuring clinical-grade reliability.

However, the IUGC 2025 dataset presents significant challenges in terms of fetal pose diversity, image quality variation, and label scarcity, limiting the effectiveness of traditional fully supervised methods in fully unlocking its clinical value. Therefore, there is an urgent need for a training strategy that can efficiently utilize the limited labeled samples along with the large amount of unlabeled images, in order to fully unlock the potential of this dataset in intrapartum assessment. Semi-Supervised Learning (SSL) provides a promising solution for such tasks, with major approaches including consistency regularization (e.g., FixMatch [3], MixMatch [4], ReMixMatch [5], UniMatch [6]) and pseudo-labeling strategies. Among these, pseudo-labeling methods such as Noisy Student [7] employ an iterative self-training paradigm, where a teacher model generates high-quality pseudo labels, which are then used to train a student model for further performance improvement. This approach introduces input noise (e.g., RandAugment [8]) and architectural noise (e.g., Stochastic Depth [9], Dropout [10]) into the student model, and gradually increases both model capacity and perturbation strength during training. It has achieved remarkable success in natural image classification tasks.

To address these challenges, we employ a DenseUNet model (as shown in Fig. 2) with heatmap regression and introduce the Noisy Student framework for semi-supervised training. The overall training pipeline is illustrated in Fig. 1. Initially, a teacher model is trained exclusively on the labeled data by minimizing the mean squared error (MSE) loss. Once the teacher model has been trained, it is used to generate pseudo-labels for the unlabeled images. Subsequently, self-training is performed under both input and structural noise; this stage simultaneously receives labeled and unlabeled images as input. A student model that mirrors the architecture of the teacher model is optimized to minimize a joint mean squared error (MSE) loss computed on both the labeled data and the pseudo-labeled data. After the student model is trained, it replaces the teacher model and the process proceeds to the next iteration.

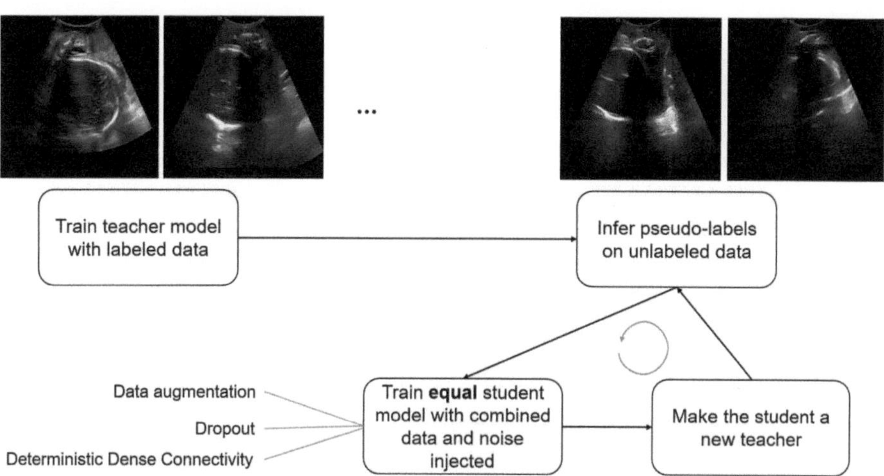

Fig. 1. The Noisy Student training pipeline used for landmark detection in intrapartum ultrasound.

To effectively enhance the generalization ability and training stability of the model in the fetal keypoint detection task, we introduce targeted improvements to the two noise mechanisms in the Noisy Student (NS) [7] framework. In terms of model noise design, we fully leverage the dense connectivity pattern of the Dense Block in DenseNet [11], whose multi-path structure inherently provides a regularization effect similar to Stochastic Depth [9]. Building upon this, we introduce Dropout [10] layers in the decoder as the primary regularization mechanism, enhancing model generalization while avoiding training instability that may arise from structural complexity. In terms of input noise design, we employ data augmentation methods tailored for medical ultrasound images and further propose a MixUp [12] augmentation strategy integrated with heatmap regression. The mixing weight coefficient in this strategy decays linearly throughout the training process, allowing the model to be exposed to stronger perturbations in the early training stages and gradually transition to a more stable phase, thereby enhancing model robustness.

Our main contributions can be summarized as follows:

1. We propose a semi-supervised learning framework based on the Noisy Student paradigm and successfully apply it to the task of fetal keypoint detection in labor ultrasound, providing a novel approach for medical image analysis in scenarios with limited annotations.
2. We propose a collaborative noise injection mechanism that enhances the model's robustness to internal randomness by jointly leveraging the dense connectivity characteristics of DenseNet and Dropout in the decoder.

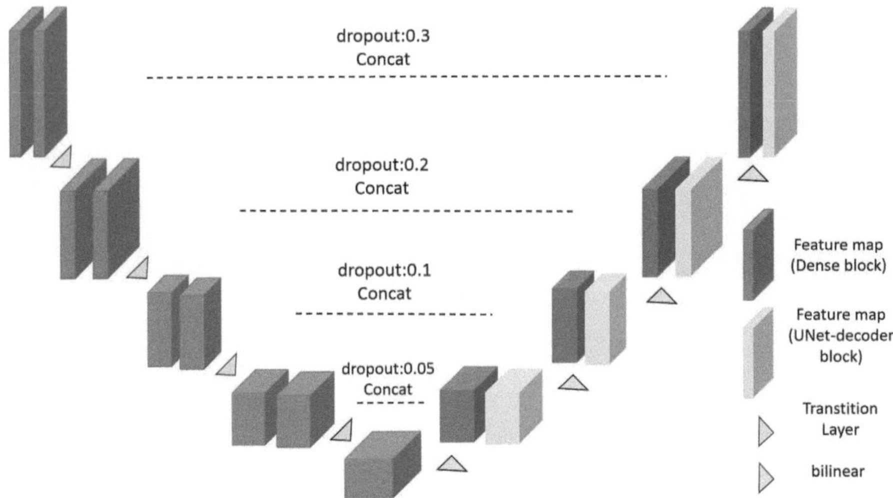

Fig. 2. Network architecture of DenseUNet.

3. We introduce a dynamic MixUp augmentation strategy, whose perturbation strength linearly decays during training and is co-optimized with the heatmap regression objective, thereby enabling stable improvement in keypoint localization accuracy.

2   Methods

The overall framework of the proposed method is illustrated in Fig. 1, following the Noisy Student paradigm for semi-supervised keypoint detection in intrapartum ultrasound images. The process involves iterative training of a teacher model and a student model.

2.1   Teacher Model Training and Pseudo-label Generation

First, the teacher model is initialized and trained on the labeled dataset $\mathcal{D}_l$. A DenseUNet architecture is employed, and the model is optimized by minimizing the Mean Squared Error (MSE) loss between the predicted heatmap H_{pred} and the ground truth heatmap H_{gt}:

$$\mathcal{L}_{teacher} = \frac{1}{N_l} \sum_{i=1}^{N_l} \|H_{pred}^i - H_{gt}^i\|_2^2 \tag{1}$$

where N_l denotes the number of labeled samples. After the teacher model is fully trained, its weights are frozen and it is used to generate pseudo-labels $\hat{H}_{pseudo}$ for the unlabeled dataset $\mathcal{D}_u$. For each unlabeled image $x_u \in \mathcal{D}_u$, the corresponding pseudo-label is obtained via the teacher model's forward pass:

$$\hat{H}_{pseudo} = f_{teacher}(x_u) \tag{2}$$

where $f_{teacher}$ represents the inference process of the teacher model. The generated pseudo-labels are then used alongside the ground truth labels for the subsequent training of the student model.

2.2 Linearly-Decaying MixUp Augmentation for Heatmap Regression

The core idea of MixUp is to generate new training samples and corresponding soft labels by linearly interpolating between two randomly selected samples (images and their labels). In the context of keypoint detection, this is realized as follows. Let two randomly selected ultrasound frames be $\mathbf{I}_A, \mathbf{I}_B \in \mathbb{R}^{H \times W \times C}$, with corresponding keypoint annotations $\mathcal{K}_A = \{(x_i^A, y_i^A)\}_{i=1}^N$, $\mathcal{K}_B = \{(x_i^B, y_i^B)\}_{i=1}^N$, where N denotes the number of anatomical landmarks. A mixing coefficient is sampled from a Beta distribution $\lambda \sim \text{Beta}(\alpha, \alpha)$, with hyper-parameter $\alpha > 0$ controlling the interpolation strength. The mixed image and keypoint coordinates are then computed as

$$\mathbf{I}_{\text{mix}} = \lambda \mathbf{I}_A + (1 - \lambda) \mathbf{I}_B, \tag{3}$$

$$(x_i^{\text{mix}}, y_i^{\text{mix}}) = \lambda (x_i^A, y_i^A) + (1 - \lambda) (x_i^B, y_i^B), \quad \forall i \in \{1, \ldots, N\}. \tag{4}$$

Consequently, the synthetic sample $(\mathbf{I}_{\text{mix}}, \mathcal{K}_{\text{mix}})$ exhibits smooth transitions in both appearance and geometry, effectively expanding the local neighborhood of the data distribution.

In our work, we adopt a heatmap regression-based keypoint detection approach, which is particularly well-suited for the soft-label formulation introduced by MixUp. Heatmaps inherently represent keypoint locations as dense, continuous 2D probability distributions. This characteristic aligns naturally with the interpolation mechanism of MixUp, enabling the mixed heatmap labels to be generated through the same linear interpolation process applied to the images and keypoint coordinates, thereby preserving spatial consistency. Moreover, heatmaps incorporate a certain degree of spatial uncertainty via a Gaussian kernel, which allows them to absorb and express the additional "blurring" effect introduced by MixUp—specifically, when keypoint positions lie between two true locations. Compared to direct coordinate regression, this heatmap-based approach demonstrates greater robustness to positional variations, thereby enhancing the model's generalization capability.

To align with the learning objectives at different training stages, we employ a linearly decaying MixUp augmentation strategy. In the early stages of training, introducing moderate data augmentation helps the model learn more robust feature representations. This is particularly important for addressing the inherent speckle noise, low contrast, and significant variations in fetal pose commonly

---

Algorithm 1: PyTorch-like pseudocode for our MixUp method

```python
1  # Input:
2  # - images I: Batch of input image tensors (B, C, H, W).
3  # - heatmaps H: Corresponding heatmap tensors (B, K, H,
       W).
4  # - landmarks L: Corresponding landmark tensors (B, 2K).
5  # - mixup parameter alpha: Beta distribution parameter.
6  # Output:
7  # - mixed_images: Mixed images tensor (B, C, H, W).
8  # - mixed_heatmaps: Mixed heatmaps tensor (B, 2K, H, W).
9  # - mixed_landmarks: Mixed landmarks tensor (B, 2, 2K).
10 # - mixed_weights: Mixing weights tensor (B, 2).
11
12 def mixup_data(images, heatmaps, landmarks, alpha=0.2,
       device='cuda'):
13     # Sample mixing coefficient from Beta distribution
14     lam = np.random.beta(alpha, alpha) if alpha > 0 else
           1.0
15     # Randomly permute batch indices
16     index = torch.randperm(images.size(0), device=device
           )
17     # Mix images using linear interpolation
18     mixed_images = lam * images + (1 - lam) * images[
           index]
19     # Mix heatmaps
20     mixed_heatmaps = torch.cat([lam * heatmaps, (1 - lam
           ) * heatmaps[index]], dim=1)
21     # Stack landmarks
22     mixed_landmarks = torch.stack([landmarks, landmarks[
           index]], dim=1)
23     # Mixing weights
24     mix_weights = torch.tensor([lam, 1 - lam], device=
           device).repeat(images.size(0), 1)
25     return mixed_images, mixed_heatmaps, mixed_landmarks
           , mix_weights
```

---

present in ultrasound images. The mixed samples during this stage also assist the model in developing an understanding of the regions and general shapes associated with anatomical keypoints. In the later stages of training, we gradually reduce the intensity of MixUp augmentation, enabling the model to focus on fine-tuning keypoint localization and achieving sub-pixel accuracy. Maintaining high localization precision at this stage is critical. Applying strong mixing strategies when the model is approaching convergence may introduce ambiguous labels or distort spatial structures, which can interfere with the learning of precise keypoint positions. The proposed decaying mechanism effectively mitigates this issue by adaptively adjusting the augmentation strength according to the training progress. We provide the corresponding pseudo-algorithm description Algorithm 1.

3   Experiments

3.1   Dataset and Implementation Details

Participants in the MICCAI IUGC 2025 challenge are provided with 300 annotated ultrasound images and 31,421 unannotated images. Additionally, 2,045 unlabeled standard AOP-plane images are released as exemplars; these exemplars are exclusively drawn from the unannotated pool and are intended to reflect the overall distribution of the unlabeled data.During the model training, all models are implemented using PyTorch and trained on a single NVIDIA Tesla 4090 GPU. The standard deviation of the Gaussian heatmap is set to $\sigma = 6$. During training, the following eleven data augmentation operations are applied: rotation, scaling, translation, brightness adjustment, Gaussian blur, gamma contrast, elastic transformation, image inversion, Cutout, and Coarse Dropout. During training, pixel-wise mean squared error (MSE) is adopted as the loss function for optimization, and the Euclidean distance between predicted and ground truth keypoints on the validation set is used as the evaluation metric for model performance, with only the best-performing parameters being saved. During inference, the DARK post-processing method is introduced as a debiasing strategy to further enhance the robustness and localization accuracy of the predictions (Table 1).

Table 1. Data augmentation methods and their parameters used in the HeatmapLandmarkDataset

Augmentation method	Parameters
Rotation	Range: -5 to $5°$
Scale	Range: $(1 - 0.125)$ to $(1 + 0.125)$
Translation	X-axis: $[-30, 30]$, Y-axis: $[-20, 20]$ pixels
Brightness adjustment	Multiplication factor range: $(1 - 0.6)$ to $(1 + 0.6)$
Gaussian blur	Applied with probability 0.1, sigma range: $(0, 1.5)$
Gamma contrast	Adjustment range: $(0.3, 2.0)$
Elastic transformation	Alpha range: $(0, 400)$, sigma fixed at 30
Image inversion	Applied with probability 0.1
Cutout	Iterations: 0 or 1, size range: 0.04 to 0.3 of image width/height, non-square cutouts
Coarse dropout	Rate: 0.02, area size: 8% of image size

3.2   Model Selection and Hyperparameter Tuning

During the model selection and hyperparameter tuning phase, we conducted experiments based on a U-shaped network with an encoder-decoder architecture. In the initial stage, we first adopted a baseline UNet model to perform module adjustments and hyperparameter optimization (as shown in Table 2). After determining the optimal hyperparameter configuration, we selected the best-performing backbone network based on this configuration (as shown in Table 3).

Table 2. Results of module adjustment and hyperparameter tuning

Method	Distance ↓	AOP_MAE ↓
b0 (*lr*: 0.0001; σ: 2; step_size: 15; γ: 0.9)	33.54	16.63
b1 (*lr*: 0.0001; σ: 3; step_size: 10; γ: 0.9)	28.88	11.43
b2 (*lr*: 0.0001; σ: 6; step_size: 10; γ: 0.9)	25.49	8.24
b3 (b2 + more aug data; step_size: 10; γ: 0.9)	22.51	8.62
b4 (b3 + decoder-dropout: [0.05, 0.1, 0.2, 0.3])	21.67	8.32
b5 (σ: 4)	25.14	8.67
b6 (γ: 0.75)	28.24	11.11
b7 (step_size: 8)	31.11	12.22
b8 (b2 + supervise the 3rd and 4th layer outputs)	24.83	8.54
b9 (b3 + ConvBlock: InstanceNorm + LeakyReLU)	22.47	8.77
b10 (b3 + ConvBlock: InstanceNorm + PReLU [13])	23.25	8.09
b11 (b3 + ConvBlock: BatchNorm + PReLU [13])	24.50	8.36
b12 (b3 + DARK [14])	20.45	7.34

As shown in Table 2, the following explains how to read the table. First, the table should be read from top to bottom. Our experimental exploration starts from the initial baseline b0, and new modules or hyperparameters are gradually introduced on this basis. Whenever a newly added module or adjusted hyperparameter configuration yields better performance than the previous baseline, it is established as the new baseline and highlighted in the table. If a row's description does not explicitly mention a reference baseline, it means the configuration is derived from the immediately preceding baseline with parameter modifications. For example, b5 is modified from b4, b6 is based on b5, and b7 further improves upon b6. Through this step-by-step optimization process, we ultimately determine b12 as the optimal configuration, which is then adopted as the hyperparameter setting for all subsequent experiments. In the table, `sigma` denotes the standard deviation σ used for generating Gaussian heatmaps, while `step_size` and γ are the step size and decay factor of the StepLR learning rate scheduler, respectively. In the table, ConvBlock refers to the ConvBlock used in the UNet decoder.

Given that our network adopts a U-shaped encoder-decoder architecture, guided by baseline b12 in Table 2, we trained multiple different backbones to determine the optimal choices for the teacher and student models. As shown in Table 3, DenseNet121 [11] achieved the best performance and was therefore selected as the final backbone for our encoder.

Table 3. Performance comparison of different backbone networks on the IUGC dataset

Backbone	Distance ↓	AOP_MAE ↓
UNet [15]	23.70	9.04
PVT-v2-b1 [16]	20.99	5.87
PVT-v2-b2 [16]	19.06	5.60
ResNet18d [17]	26.16	7.59
ConvNeXtv2-Tiny [18]	15.51	6.63
ResNet34 [17]	25.11	8.01
seresnext26d_32x4d [19]	20.75	7.02
DenseNet121 [11]	18.08	5.99
DenseNet161 [11]	18.64	6.24

3.3 Pseudo-label Filtering

We first perform 5-fold cross-validation on 300 annotated images (240 for training and 60 for validation) and construct a UNet model with DenseNet121 as the backbone to train the teacher model. Based on the two best-performing models on the validation set, we conduct inference on the 2,045 unlabeled images, initially setting the pseudo-label selection threshold to a maximum heatmap activation value of no less than 0.7.

However, due to artifacts, acoustic shadows, and low contrast in ultrasound images, the response magnitude becomes decoupled from localization accuracy: high-confidence false positives may arise at incorrect locations, while true positives at correct landmarks are erroneously filtered out due to weak signals (loss of low-confidence true positives). Moreover, variations in echogenicity across structures cause a uniform threshold to systematically favor "easy-to-detect" landmarks (e.g., the pubic symphysis), while neglecting clinically critical yet challenging structures, thereby exacerbating class imbalance. To this end, we explored an uncertainty-based pseudo-labeling paradigm, for example, an entropy-based correction strategy incorporating temperature scaling sharpness and per-landmark adaptive thresholds, to mitigate the confidence bias issue. However, due to its implementation complexity and difficulty in achieving stable convergence under the current data conditions, this approach was ultimately not successfully deployed.

The configuration `pse825_1e260` trains the model using 825 pseudo-labeled images generated via the pseudo-labeling technique and 260 fully annotated images. Building upon this, `pse825_se_165_1e260` incorporates an additional 165 pseudo-labeled images derived from the original unlabeled pool, while keeping the number of annotated images fixed at 260. Similarly, `pse825_se_100_1e260` and `pse825_se_100_1e220` both introduce pseudo-labels from 100 selected unlabeled images; however, the former uses 260 annotated images, whereas the latter reduces the number of annotated images to 220, aiming to evaluate the compensatory capability of pseudo-labels when labeled data is reduced., aiming to

Table 4. Comparison of different training-data compositions on the IUGC dataset

Training data	Distance ↓	AOP_MAE ↓
pse825_1e260	18.35	6.85
pse825_se_165_le260	18.27	6.74
pse825_se_100_le260	17.96	6.57
pse825_se_100_1e220	18.24	5.58

Table 5. Comparison of different training-data with mixup compositions on the IUGC dataset.

Training data	Distance ↓	AOP_MAE ↓
pse825_1e260	17.67	5.06
pse825_se_165_le260	17.43	5.10
pse825_se_100_le260	16.29	5.47
pse825_se_100_1e220	16.35	4.94

evaluate the compensatory capability of pseudo-labeling when labeled data is reduced.

As a compromise, we designed a multi-threshold filtering strategy: we first identified high-confidence samples using higher thresholds 0.7, then excluded these from the pseudo-labels generated under a lower threshold (0.6), retaining moderate-confidence candidates with broader spatial coverage. This yielded 825 pseudo-labeled images with more comprehensive representation. Further analysis revealed a significant number of redundant samples with similar imaging angles, which could lead to overfitting. Therefore, we randomly divided these 825 images into five non-overlapping subsets, to be used for training. Furthermore, to reduce redundancy in the annotated data, we removed 40 highly similar samples from the original 260 annotated images and transferred them to the validation set. Finally, the student model's training set consists of 220 annotated images and

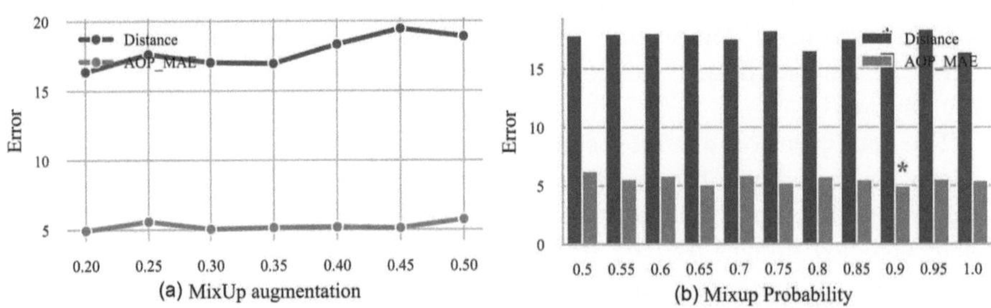

Fig. 3. Impact of MixUp application augmentation and probability on distance and AOP-MAE.

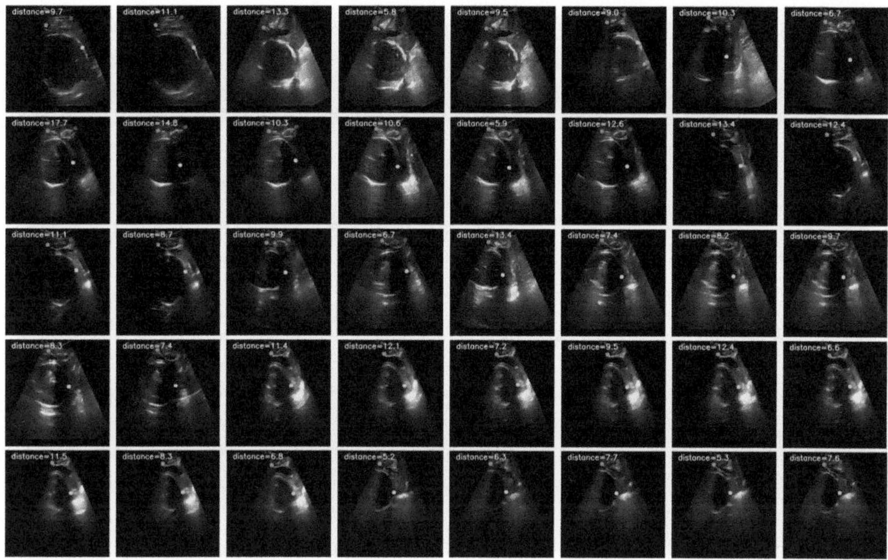

Fig. 4. Visualization of the final ensemble model's predictions on validation set samples. The predicted keypoint locations on the input images are shown, where red dots indicate PS1, green dots indicate PS2, and yellow dots indicate FH1. The distance difference (distance) between the predicted results and the ground truth labels is annotated in the top-left corner of each image.

100 high-quality pseudo-labeled images. This strategy led to a modest improvement in model performance, as shown in Table 4. Based on the aforementioned dataset and with the Mixup augmentation strength set to 0.2, we further evaluate the impact of different training data combinations on the performance of the student model, with specific results presented in Table 5. Notably, the models under the configurations **pse825_se100_le220** and **pse825_se100_le260** exhibit particularly outstanding performance. We therefore choose to ensemble the models corresponding to the best weights obtained under these two configurations and visualize the predictions of this ensemble model on the validation set used during local training, as shown in Fig. 4. Subsequently, this ensemble model is submitted as the final test model for the IUGC 2025 challenge. On the IUGC 2025 official validation set, the ensemble model achieves Distance and AOP_MAE scores of 15.85 and 5.14, respectively, and further improves to 13.16 and 4.42 on the independent test set.

On the pse825_se100_le220 training dataset, we conducted experiments on the strength of Mixup augmentation, with results shown in subplot (a) of Fig. 3. The results indicate that the model achieves optimal performance when the Mixup strength is set to 0.2. This is primarily because this strength value strikes a good balance between preserving keypoint spatial accuracy and enhancing model generalization: under this setting, the mixed samples generated by Mixup can better retain the clear structure of the original images, effectively avoiding blurring or distortion of keypoints caused by excessive interpolation; at the same time, the moderate introduction of data diversity helps alleviate overfitting in small-sample scenarios, thereby improving model robustness. Building upon the determination that the optimal Mixup strength is 0.2, we further adjusted its application probability (as shown subplot (b) of Fig. 3, where the best result is marked with a red star). All experiments set the minimum application probability of Mixup to 0.1 to ensure that the model can converge more stably as training approaches the end.

4   Conclusion

This study proposes a semi-supervised learning method based on the Noisy Student framework to address the issue of insufficient accuracy in fetal anatomical landmark detection from labor ultrasound images. We construct a Dense-UNet model with DenseNet121 as the encoder and introduce a linearly decaying MixUp data augmentation strategy specifically designed for heatmap regression during training, effectively enhancing the model's robustness and generalization capability. On the competition dataset containing 34,421 images, our method achieved significant performance improvement by using only 220 labeled images and an additional 100 carefully selected unlabeled images for training. Experimental results demonstrate that the Noisy Student training framework can effectively leverage the value of unlabeled data even under extremely limited labeling conditions, revealing its potential for fetal keypoint detection in labor ultrasound.

Acknowledgements. This work was supported in part by the Research and Practice Project of Research Teaching Reform in Henan Undergraduate University under Grant 2022SYJXLX114, in part by the Key Research Programs of Higher Education Institutions in Henan Province under Grant 24B520026 and 25A520041, and in part by the Special Research Project for the Construction of Provincial Demonstration Schools at Nanyang Institute of Technology under Grant SFX202314, and in part by the Interdisciplinary Sciences Project, Nanyang Institute of Technology.

The authors have no competing interests to declare that are relevant to the content of this article.

References

1. Bai, J., et al.: Landmark detection challenge for intrapartum ultrasound measurement meeting the actual clinical assessment of labor progress (2025). https://doi.org/10.5281/zenodo.15172238
2. Bai, J., et al.: Intrapartum ultrasound grand challenge 2024 (2024). https://doi.org/10.5281/zenodo.10979813
3. Sohn, K., et al.: FixMatch: simplifying semi-supervised learning with consistency and confidence (2020). https://arxiv.org/abs/2001.07685
4. Berthelot, D., Carlini, N., Goodfellow, I., Papernot, N., Oliver, A., Raffel, C.: MixMatch: a holistic approach to semi-supervised learning (2019). https://arxiv.org/abs/1905.02249

5. Berthelot, D., et al.: Remixmatch: semi-supervised learning with distribution matching and augmentation anchoring. In: International Conference on Learning Representations (2020). https://openreview.net/forum?id=HklkeR4KPB

6. Li, R., et al.: UniMatch: universal matching from atom to task for few-shot drug discovery. In: The Thirteenth International Conference on Learning Representations (2025). https://openreview.net/forum?id=v9EjwMM55Y

7. Xie, Q., Luong, M.T., Hovy, E., Le, Q.V.: Self-training with noisy student improves ImageNet classification (2020). https://arxiv.org/abs/1911.04252

8. Cubuk, E.D., Zoph, B., Shlens, J., Le, Q.: Randaugment: practical automated data augmentation with a reduced search space. In: Larochelle, H., Ranzato, M., Hadsell, R., Balcan, M., Lin, H. (eds.) Advances in Neural Information Processing Systems, vol. 33, pp. 18613–18624. Curran Associates, Inc. (2020). https://proceedings.neurips.cc/paper_files/paper/2020/file/d85b63ef0ccb114d0a3bb7b7d808028f-Paper.pdf

9. Huang, G., Sun, Y., Liu, Z., Sedra, D., Weinberger, K.: Deep networks with stochastic depth (2016). https://arxiv.org/abs/1603.09382

10. Gal, Y., Ghahramani, Z.: Dropout as a Bayesian approximation: representing model uncertainty in deep learning (2016). https://arxiv.org/abs/1506.02142

11. Huang, G., Liu, Z., Van Der Maaten, L., Weinberger, K.Q.: Densely connected convolutional networks. In: 2017 IEEE Conference on Computer Vision and Pattern Recognition (CVPR), pp. 2261–2269 (2017). https://doi.org/10.1109/CVPR.2017.243

12. Zhang, H., Cisse, M., Dauphin, Y.N., Lopez-Paz, D.: mixup: beyond empirical risk minimization. In: International Conference on Learning Representations (2018). https://openreview.net/forum?id=r1Ddp1-Rb

13. Pinto, R.C., Tavares, A.R.: PReLU: yet another single-layer solution to the XOR problem (2024). https://arxiv.org/abs/2409.10821

14. Zhang, F., Zhu, X., Dai, H., Ye, M., Zhu, C.: Distribution-aware coordinate representation for human pose estimation (2019). https://arxiv.org/abs/1910.06278

15. Ronneberger, O., Fischer, P., Brox, T.: U-Net: convolutional networks for biomedical image segmentation (2015). https://arxiv.org/abs/1505.04597

16. Wang, W., et al.: PVT v2: improved baselines with pyramid vision transformer. Comput. Vis. Media 1–10 (2022). https://doi.org/10.1007/s41095-022-0274-8

17. He, K., Zhang, X., Ren, S., Sun, J.: Deep residual learning for image recognition (2015). https://arxiv.org/abs/1512.03385

18. Woo, S., et al.: ConvNeXt v2: co-designing and scaling ConvNets with masked autoencoders (2023). https://arxiv.org/abs/2301.00808

19. Xie, S., Girshick, R., Dollár, P., Tu, Z., He, K.: Aggregated residual transformations for deep neural networks (2017). https://arxiv.org/abs/1611.05431

Unlabeled Data-Driven Fetal Landmark Detection in Intrapartum Ultrasound

Chen Ma, Yunshu Li, Bowen Guo, Jing Jiao, Yi Huang,
Yuanyuan Wang, and Yi Guo(✉)

Fudan University, Shanghai, China
guoyi@fudan.edu.cn

Abstract. The angle of progression (AoP) is a critical parameter for assessing fetal head descent during labor, requiring identification of three anatomical landmarks in intrapartum ultrasound images. Manual annotation is time-consuming and prone to inter- and intra-observer variability, while automated methods are hindered by limited labeled data and domain shifts across ultrasound devices. We propose an automated fetal biometry method for AoP calculation based on a modified TransUNet architecture with TinyViT backbone. The design integrates (i) MAE-assisted knowledge distillation from an Ultrasound Foundation Model (USFM) for robust representation learning, (ii) label perturbation to enhance robustness and cross-device generalization, and (iii) semi-supervised learning with pseudo-labeling to leverage unlabeled data. The network predicts heatmaps for landmark localization and calculates AoP from the detected coordinates. On the IUGC2025 Challenge test set, the proposed method achieved a mean radial error of 11.6749 pixels and a mean absolute AoP error of 3.8061 degrees.

Keywords: Intrapartum Ultrasound · Angle of Progression · Keypoint Detection · Pseudo Labels · Model Pretraining

1 Introduction

Labor monitoring is essential for ensuring maternal and fetal safety during childbirth. The World Health Organization's Labour Care Guide (LCG) emphasizes the importance of systematic assessment of fetal head position and progression for timely clinical decision-making. Among the critical parameters, the angle of progression (AoP) measured from intrapartum ultrasound provides crucial insights into fetal descent and directly influences intervention decisions [6,12]. The AoP is calculated by identifying three anatomical landmarks: two points along the pubic symphysis (PS1, PS2) and one point where a tangent from PS1 touches the fetal head (FH1).

In recent years, deep learning has shown great promise for analyzing intrapartum ultrasound images, particularly for pubic symphysis and fetal head segmentation. Traditional approaches generally follow a two-stage pipeline: first segmenting the anatomical structures, then calculating the angle of progression. Lu

© The Author(s), under exclusive license to Springer Nature Switzerland AG 2026
J. Bai et al. (Eds.): IUGC 2025, LNCS 16317, pp. 14–23, 2026.
https://doi.org/10.1007/978-3-032-11616-1_2

et al. [14] proposed a multitask deep neural network combining image segmentation, endpoint detection, and angle calculation using a shared encoder with multiple decoders. Bai et al. [1] developed a dual-branch network for computing AoP from transperineal ultrasound images. Chen et al. [5] introduced direction-guided and multi-scale feature screening methods for improved segmentation-based AoP computation. Chen et al. [4] proposed a dual-path boundary-guided residual network (DBRN) with attention mechanisms. Furthermore, Ou et al. [15] developed RTSeg-Net, a lightweight model for real-time fetal headpubic symphysis segmentation in clinical settings.

Despite recent progress, segmentation-first pipelines face notable limitations. First, the multi-stage process enables errors from the segmentation step to propagate to landmark localization and AoP calculation, ultimately degrading final accuracy. Second, segmentation requires dense pixel-level annotations, which are costly to obtain and prone to inter-observer variability. These drawbacks motivate the exploration of direct landmark detection, which can mitigate error accumulation, reduce annotation burden, and improve computational efficiency.

However, direct landmark detection in intrapartum ultrasound introduces its own challenges. The images are inherently noisy with low contrast [7], and substantial domain shifts across devices and manufacturers hinder model generalization [2,18]. In addition, expert landmark annotation is time-consuming, and the scarcity of labeled datasets makes it difficult to train robust models, especially under cross-device variations.

To address these challenges, we propose a novel automated fetal biometry method for AoP calculation that integrates self-supervised pretraining, lightweight architecture design, and cross-device adaptation.

The main contributions of this paper are as follows:

- A MAE-assisted knowledge distillation framework using USFM as teacher to train a lightweight TinyViT backbone specifically adapted for intrapartum ultrasound;
- A modified TransUNet architecture combining ResNet-50 encoder, transformer bottleneck, and UNet decoder for precise heatmap-based landmark detection;
- Training strategies incorporating cross-device adaptation through label perturbation and semi-supervised learning via iterative pseudo-labeling to leverage abundant unlabeled data.

Our method achieves superior performance compared to baseline approaches, with mean radial error of 11.6749 pixels and absolute parameter difference of 3.8061 degrees on the test set, demonstrating significant potential to streamline clinical workflows and improve diagnostic consistency in intrapartum care.

2   Methods

2.1   Overview

Our approach for automated fetal biometry in intrapartum ultrasound images consists of three main components: (1) a pretraining phase leveraging MAE-assisted knowledge distillation to learn domain-specific features from intrapartum ultrasound data, (2) a modified TransUNet architecture for keypoint detection, and (3) training strategies that incorporate cross-device adaptation and semi-supervised learning. This methodology is designed to address the core challenges of limited labeled data, cross-device generalization, and the spatial relationship modeling crucial for accurate anatomical landmark detection.

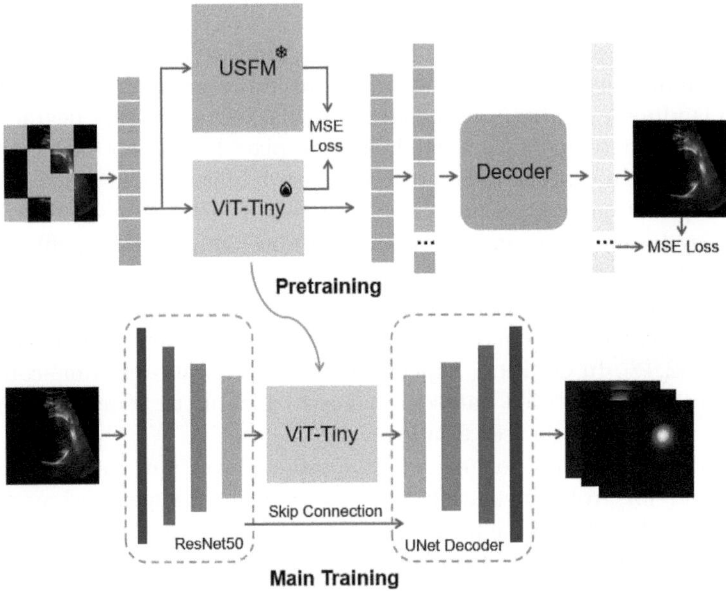

Fig. 1. Overview of the Pretraining Phase and Main Training Phase

2.2   Model Pretraining

To meet the demands of accurate and real-time keypoint detection in intrapartum ultrasound, we adopt a compact TinyViT backbone enhanced via MAE-assisted knowledge distillation, as shown in the upper part of Fig. 1. Specifically, the Ultrasound Foundation Model (USFM) [10] serves as the teacher network, transferring domain-specific anatomical representations to the lightweight student model.

The MAE pretraining method [8], which reconstructs masked image patches, is particularly suited for heatmap-based keypoint detection, as it captures spatial dependencies across image regions and facilitates precise landmark localization. This formulation also enables effective utilization of unlabeled intrapartum ultrasound images to enrich the learned representations.

The overall distillation loss is defined as:

$$\mathcal{L}_{distill} = MSE(f_{student}(x), f_{teacher}(x)) + \lambda \mathcal{L}_{MAE}(x_{masked}) \qquad (1)$$

where $f_{student}$ and $f_{teacher}$ represent the feature extraction functions of the TinyViT and USFM models respectively, and L_{MAE} is the masked autoencoder reconstruction loss.

The resulting TinyViT model serves as the backbone for our keypoint detection network, providing a computationally efficient yet powerful feature extractor that has been specifically adapted to the characteristics of transperineal ultrasound images.

2.3   Network Architecture

Our keypoint detection model builds on a modified TransUNet [3] architecture that integrates a ResNet-50 [9] backbone encoder, a ViT-style transformer bottleneck using a distilled TinyViT [17], and a UNet-like decoder with skip connections, designed to predict heatmaps for anatomical landmark localization in intrapartum ultrasound images. As shown in the lower half of Fig. 1, the model structure is mainly divided into the following parts.

Encoder. The encoder employs a ResNet-50 pretrained backbone to extract hierarchical feature maps at multiple scales. This multi-scale representation provides rich local details from shallow layers and abstract semantic information from deeper layers, facilitating precise anatomical localization.

TinyViT Bottleneck. The last encoder layer is projected to a lower-dimensional embedding and then fed into the pretrained TinyViT from Sect. 2.2 for further processing. The output tokens are reshaped back into spatial features for decoding.

Decoder. The decoder reconstructs high-resolution feature maps through a series of transposed convolutional upsampling layers. At each upsampling stage, features are concatenated with the corresponding encoder features via skip connections to fuse local and global information effectively. Each concatenated feature map is refined by a lightweight double convolution block composed of two sequential convolution, batch normalization, and ReLU activation layers. The decoder progressively upsamples features until the spatial resolution matches the desired heatmap size.

Output Head and Coordinate Extraction. A final 1×1 convolution layer projects the decoder's output to K heatmaps ($K = 3$ in our case), each representing the predicted spatial probability distribution of one anatomical landmark. The heatmaps have a fixed spatial resolution of 64×64. Landmark coordinates are extracted by locating the spatial maxima of each heatmap via an argmax operation, followed by normalization to relative coordinates.

Loss Funtion. The model is trained using a single heatmap loss:

$$\mathcal{L}_{heatmap} = MSE(heatmap_{pred}, heatmap_{gt}) \qquad (2)$$

where $heatmap_{pred}$, and $heatmap_{gt}$ denote the predicted and ground-truth heatmaps, respectively. The loss is computed as mean squared error (MSE) between them.

2.4   Training Strategies

Device-Domain Adaption. The dataset presents a significant domain shift, as the training images are acquired from two ultrasound machines, whereas the test set consists of images from two different devices. To improve the model's robustness across domains, we apply label perturbation during training by injecting Gaussian noise into the ground truth landmark coordinates:

$$(\tilde{x}_i, \tilde{y}_i) = (x_i, y_i) + \mathcal{N}(0, \sigma^2 I) \qquad (3)$$

where $\sigma = 2$ pixels. This perturbation acts as a regularizer, encouraging the network to learn features that are invariant to small spatial variations caused by differences in machine calibration and imaging protocols, thus enhancing generalization to unseen domains.

Pseudo Labeling. Given the substantial imbalance between labeled and unlabeled images, we employ iterative pseudo-labeling to leverage the abundant unlabeled data. We generate pseudo-labels using the device-domain-adapted model and select high-quality samples based on multiple criteria: (1) prediction confidence measured by heatmap peak sharpness and (2) geometric plausibility enforcing anatomical constraints between landmarks.

3   Experiments

3.1   Datasets

The challenge organizers provide a training set comprising 300 labeled intrapartum ultrasound images, each annotated with three anatomical landmarks (PS1, PS2, FH1) and the angle of progression (AoP). The corresponding annotations are stored in a CSV file containing the image filenames, landmark coordinates (x, y), and AoP values. In addition, the dataset includes 31,421 unlabeled intrapartum ultrasound images. To facilitate standard-plane identification, 2,045 reference images depicting the standard acquisition view are also provided.

We further incorporate the FH-PS-AoP public dataset [11], containing 4,000 annotated intrapartum ultrasound images at a native resolution of 256×256, for model pretraining. The detailed data statistics are shown in Table 1.

For each main training phase, the available labeled data are randomly split into training and test subsets with a ratio of 4:1.

Table 1. Summary of datasets used in this study

Dataset	# Images	Annotations	Resolution
Labeled cases	300	PS1, PS2, FH1, AoP	512×512
Unlabeled cases	31,421	None	512×512
Standard-plane examples	2,045	None	512×512
FH-PS-AoP	4,000	None	256×256

Preprocessing. All images are resized to 224×224 during pretraining. For main training and evaluation phases, images are resized to 512×512, and landmark coordinates are scaled accordingly.

For each annotated landmark, we generate a Gaussian heatmap representation to serve as the regression target. Given the landmark location (x_0, y_0), the heatmap H at pixel location (x, y) is defined as:

$$H(x, y) = exp(-\frac{(x - x_0)^2 + (y - y_0)^2}{2\sigma^2}) \tag{4}$$

where $\sigma = 4$ pixels controls the spatial spread. This continuous spatial encoding provides localized supervision, allowing the network to learn more precise keypoint localization compared to direct coordinate regression.

Data Augmentation. To improve robustness to acquisition variability and mitigate overfitting, we employ both geometric and photometric augmentations.

Geometric: In-plane rotations, and random scaling with cropping are applied jointly to images and landmark coordinates to preserve spatial alignment, with AoP values recalculated from the transformed points.

Photometric: Gamma correction and contrast adjustment are applied to simulate device- and operator-induced appearance variations, without altering landmark positions.

This augmentation strategy strengthens the model's resilience to spatial perturbations and intensity variations, facilitating cross-device generalization in intrapartum ultrasound analysis.

3.2   Experimental Settings

During the pretraining phase, we set the probability of spatial domain masking at 0.75 and employed the AdamW optimizer with an initial learning rate of 1e-4, complemented by a cosine learning rate decay strategy. The experiments were trained for 400 epochs with a batch size of 1024.

In the main training, we employed the Adam optimizer with an initial learning rate of 3e-5 and adopt a StepLR learning rate decay strategy, training for 100 epochs with a batch size of 4.

All experiments were conducted on an AMD EPYC 7763 CPU and NVIDIA A100 GPU. All models were developed using PyTorch.

4   Results and Discussion

4.1   Quantitative Results on Validation Phase

We evaluate all methods on two sets of metrics: one computed on our own test split, and another obtained from the challenge platform's validation phase. Both sets report **Mean Radial Error (MRE)**—the average Euclidean distance between predicted and ground-truth landmarks–and **Absolute Parameter Difference (APD)**—the absolute difference in the predicted AoP angle. Lower values indicate better performance.

Table 2 summarizes the results. Our proposed method consistently outperforms the baseline(a UNet [16] based model) across both test and validation sets. Pretraining on external datasets and leveraging pseudo-labels further improve accuracy, with label perturbation providing additional robustness and the best overall results. As illustrated in Fig. 2, the heatmaps generated by our method show significantly improved localization capability and reduced uncertainty compared to other models.

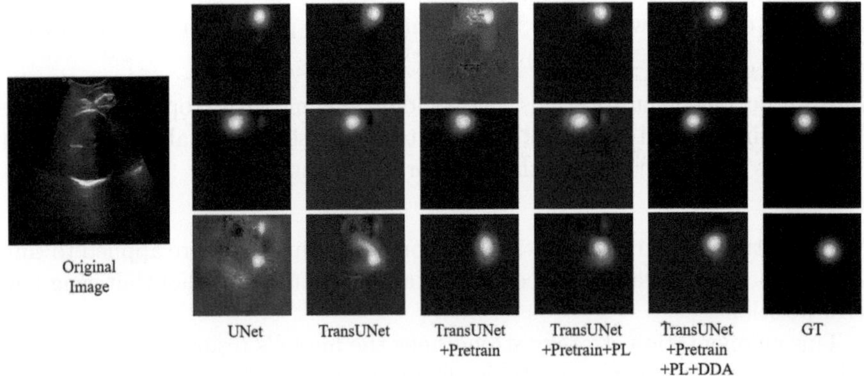

Fig. 2. Comparison of heatmaps generated by different methods.(PL: pseudo-labeling; DDA: device-domain adaptation)

4.2   Quantitative Results on Test Phase

We evaluated our final model, which incorporates pretraining, pseudo-labeling, and device-domain adaptation, on the final test phase. The performance metrics include the Mean Radial Error (MRE) between predicted and ground truth

Table 2. Comparison of different methods on test split and challenge platform validation phase. Metrics reported are Mean Radial Error (MRE) in pixels and Absolute Parameter Difference (APD) in degrees; lower is better. (PL: pseudo-labeling; DDA: device-domain adaptation)

Method	Test Split		Validation Phase	
	MRE ↓	APD ↓	MRE ↓	APD ↓
Baseline (Heatmap U-Net)	14.3266	6.2033	22.8510	8.8178
TransUNet	14.1093	5.8906	20.3387	7.4982
TransUNet + Pretrain	13.5632	5.5691	17.5204	6.6031
TransUNet + Pretrain + PL	12.8841	5.2377	15.6327	5.9873
TransUNet + Pretrain + PL + DDA	**12.3115**	**4.9815**	**14.3584**	**5.1569**

landmark points, and the Absolute Parameter Difference (APD) for the angle of progression (AoP). Results, as shown in Table 3, demonstrate that the model achieves robust and accurate landmark localization and AoP estimation on unseen test data.

Table 3. Test phase performance of the final model. Metrics reported are Mean Radial Error (MRE) in pixels and Absolute Parameter Difference (APD) in degrees; lower is better

Model	MRE ↓	APD ↓
TransUNet + Pretrain + PL + DDA	**11.6749**	**3.8061**

4.3   Limitation and Future Work

Despite the promising results, our device-domain adaptation (DDA) method exhibits some instability. This is primarily due to the random noise introduced in the label perturbation process, which can cause fluctuations in training performance and occasionally result in poor outcomes on certain samples. For example, a few images in the validation phase showed significantly degraded performance. In future work, we plan to explore more stable and robust unsupervised domain adaptation techniques to mitigate this issue.

Additionally, constrained by the inference time limitations imposed by the challenge and the need for rapid model iteration, we selected a lightweight TinyViT model as our backbone. We also experimented with larger Vision Transformer variants such as USFM and SAM [13], integrated as backbones within the TransUNet architecture. These larger models achieved performance comparable to the TinyViT model, which benefited from MAE-assisted knowledge distillation specialized for intrapartum ultrasound images, despite not undergoing the distillation process themselves. This not only validates the effectiveness of our MAE-assisted distillation strategy but also suggests that further optimizing these larger models specifically for intrapartum data may yield even better results. Future research will focus on targeted enhancements of USFM and SAM models on intrapartum ultrasound images to further boost performance.

5   Conclusion

In this paper, we proposed a unified framework for precise anatomical landmark localization and angle of progression estimation in intrapartum ultrasound images. Our method incorporates a lightweight TinyViT backbone–pretrained with knowledge distillation on USFM using related ultrasound data–integrated within a heatmap TransUNet architecture. Together with pseudo-labeling and device-domain adaptation strategies, this approach significantly enhances accuracy and generalization across varied datasets. Experimental results demonstrate strong performance and efficiency, highlighting the potential of our method for practical intrapartum ultrasound analysis.

Acknowledgments. This work was supported by the National Natural Science Foundation of China (82227803, 62371139), and the Foundation of the Shanghai Municipal Education Commission (24KXZNA09).

Disclosure of Interests. The authors have no competing interests to declare that are relevant to the content of this article.

References

1. Bai, J., et al.: A framework for computing angle of progression from transperineal ultrasound images for evaluating fetal head descent using a novel double branch network. Front. Physiol. **13**, 940150 (2022)
2. Chen, H., Ni, D., Qin, J., Li, S., Yang, X., Wang, T., Heng, P.A.: Standard plane localization in fetal ultrasound via domain transferred deep neural networks. IEEE J. Biomed. Health Inform. **19**(5), 1627–1636 (2015)
3. Chen, J., Lu, Y., Yu, Q., Luo, X., Adeli, E., Wang, Y., Lu, L., Yuille, A.L., Zhou, Y.: Transunet: Transformers make strong encoders for medical image segmentation. arXiv preprint arXiv:2102.04306 (2021)
4. Chen, Z., Lu, Y., Long, S., Campello, V.M., Bai, J., Lekadir, K.: Fetal head and pubic symphysis segmentation in intrapartum ultrasound image using a dual-path boundary-guided residual network. IEEE J. Biomed. Health Inform. **28**(8), 4648–4659 (2024)
5. Chen, Z., Ou, Z., Lu, Y., Bai, J.: Direction-guided and multi-scale feature screening for fetal head-pubic symphysis segmentation and angle of progression calculation. Expert Syst. Appl. **245**, 123096 (2024)
6. Dall'Asta, A., Angeli, L., Masturzo, B., Volpe, N., Schera, G.B.L., Di Pasquo, E., Girlando, F., Attini, R., Menato, G., Frusca, T., et al.: Prediction of spontaneous vaginal delivery in nulliparous women with a prolonged second stage of labor: the value of intrapartum ultrasound. Am. J. Obstet. Gynecol. **221**(6), 642-e1 (2019)

7. Duarte-Salazar, C.A., Castro-Ospina, A.E., Becerra, M.A., Delgado-Trejos, E.: Speckle noise reduction in ultrasound images for improving the metrological evaluation of biomedical applications: an overview. IEEE Access **8**, 15983–15999 (2020)
8. He, K., Chen, X., Xie, S., Li, Y., Dollár, P., Girshick, R.: Masked autoencoders are scalable vision learners. In: Proceedings of the IEEE/CVF Conference on Computer Vision and Pattern Recognition, pp. 16000–16009 (2022)
9. He, K., Zhang, X., Ren, S., Sun, J.: Deep residual learning for image recognition. In: Proceedings of the IEEE Conference on Computer Vision and Pattern Recognition, pp. 770–778 (2016)
10. Jiao, J., Zhou, J., Li, X., Xia, M., Huang, Y., Huang, L., Wang, N., Zhang, X., Zhou, S., Wang, Y., et al.: USFM: a universal ultrasound foundation model generalized to tasks and organs towards label efficient image analysis. Med. Image Anal. **96**, 103202 (2024)
11. Jieyun, B., ZhanHong, O.: Pubic symphysis-fetal head segmentation and angle of progression (2023). https://doi.org/10.5281/zenodo.7851339
12. Kalache, K.D., Dückelmann, A., Michaelis, S., Lange, J., Cichon, G., Dudenhausen, J.: Transperineal ultrasound imaging in prolonged second stage of labor with occipito anterior presenting fetuses: how well does the 'angle of progression' predict the mode of delivery? Ultrasound Obstet. Gynecol. **33**(3), 326–330 (2009)
13. Kirillov, A., Mintun, E., Ravi, N., Mao, H., Rolland, C., Gustafson, L., Xiao, T., Whitehead, S., Berg, A.C., Lo, W.Y., et al.: Segment anything. In: Proceedings of the IEEE/CVF International Conference on Computer Vision, pp. 4015–4026 (2023)
14. Lu, Y., Zhi, D., Zhou, M., Lai, F., Chen, G., Ou, Z., Zeng, R., Long, S., Qiu, R., Zhou, M., et al.: Multitask deep neural network for the fully automatic measurement of the angle of progression. Comput. Math. Methods Med. **2022**(1), 5192338 (2022)
15. Ou, Z., Bai, J., Chen, Z., Lu, Y., Wang, H., Long, S., Chen, G.: Rtseg-net: a lightweight network for real-time segmentation of fetal head and pubic symphysis from intrapartum ultrasound images. Comput. Biol. Med. **175**, 108501 (2024)
16. Ronneberger, O., Fischer, P., Brox, T.: U-net: convolutional networks for biomedical image segmentation. In: International Conference on Medical Image Computing and Computer-Assisted Intervention, pp. 234–241. Springer (2015)
17. Touvron, H., Cord, M., Douze, M., Massa, F., Sablayrolles, A., Jégou, H.: Training data-efficient image transformers and distillation through attention. In: International Conference on Machine Learning, pp. 10347–10357. PMLR (2021)
18. Zhou, M., Wang, C., Lu, Y., Qiu, R., Zeng, R., Zhi, D., Jiang, X., Ou, Z., Wang, H., Chen, G., et al.: The segmentation effect of style transfer on fetal head ultrasound image: a study of multi-source data. Med. Biol. Eng. Comput. **61**(5), 1017–1031 (2023)

SSL-FetalBioNet: Self-supervised Learning for Automated Angle of Progression Measurement in Intrapartum Ultrasound

Wang Kun, Li Lifei, Ma Yuzhang, Han Xiaoxin, Shao Haochen, and Wang Kun(✉)

Gansu University of Chinese medicine, Lanzhou Gansu 730000, China
995956009@qq.com

Abstract. During childbirth, real-time assessment of fetal head position and progression is crucial for ensuring the safety of both mother and infant. Detecting key anatomical landmarks in intrapartum ultrasound images and calculating the Angle of progression (AoP) have become critical techniques in the next-generation childbirth monitoring protocol proposed by the World Health Organization (WHO). However, traditional manual analysis is time-consuming and prone to subjective bias, highlighting the urgent need for automated methods to achieve standardized and precise childbirth assessment. This paper presents a key point detection approach combining self-supervised pre-training with a U-Net architecture: first, the encoder is pre-trained using large-scale unlabeled images through self-supervision to uncover latent structural information; subsequently, this pre-trained encoder is transferred to the supervised learning stage to achieve precise localization of three key points (PS1, PS2, FH1). Our method achieved eighth place in the Intrapartum Ultrasound Grand Challenge 2025, demonstrating its effectiveness and generalization capability in the task of key point detection in intrapartum ultrasound. This work provides a practical and feasible pathway toward automated and scalable childbirth monitoring, with significant implications for global maternal and infant health.

Keywords: Self-supervised Learning · U-Net · Intrapartum Ultrasound · Angle of Progress

1 Introduction

The dynamic nature of labor necessitates continuous monitoring of maternal and fetal health status in clinical practice. To standardize intrapartum monitoring and promote woman-centered childbirth experiences, the World Health Organization (WHO) [10] introduced the Labour Care Guide (LCG) in 2020, emphasizing the need for standardized measurement of key delivery parameters. The degree of fetal descent and rotation during delivery serves as crucial

J. Bai et al. (Eds.): IUGC 2025, LNCS 16317, pp. 24–32, 2026.
https://doi.org/10.1007/978-3-032-11616-1_3

indicators for assessing labor progress. The Angle of Progression (AoP), as a core parameter reflecting this process, is increasingly becoming a critical basis for clinical decisions regarding intervention timing and methods.AoP calculation relies on accurate identification of three key anatomical landmarks in intrapartum ultrasound images: the two most superior points of the pubic symphysis (PS1 and PS2) and the tangent point contacting the fetal head (FH1). However, current clinical practice predominantly depends on experienced sonographers for manual annotation of these landmarks, which is not only time-consuming and subjective but also susceptible to intra-/inter-observer variability, consequently compromising diagnostic consistency and reproducibility [8]. Therefore, developing an efficient, accurate, and automated landmark detection method is of significant importance for advancing intelligent labor assessment.In medical image processing, deep learning technologies–particularly convolutional neural network (CNN)-based models–have been widely applied to tasks such as image segmentation [1], object detection, and keypoint localization. Fully convolutional architectures like U-Net have demonstrated exceptional performance in medical image segmentation [11]. Nevertheless, acquiring annotated data remains challenging in practical applications, especially for high-quality medical imaging data, where annotation expertise and cost constraints hinder further development of supervised learning.

Self-Supervised Learning (SSL) has emerged as a vital approach to address the shortage of medical imaging data by learning useful image representations through designed pretext tasks without requiring human-generated labels. In the Intrapartum Ultrasound Grand Challenge (IUGC) 2025, the organizers provided a well-structured and comprehensive dataset comprising 300 labeled cases [2], 31,421 unlabeled cases, and 2,045 reference standard plane images. The task required automatic localization of three key landmarks and precise calculation of AoP based on transperineal ultrasound images. To encourage exploration of model generalization capabilities, the use of additional pre-trained models was permitted. Two core evaluation metrics were adopted to assess algorithm performance: Mean Radial Error (MRE) for evaluating landmark localization accuracy and Absolute Parameter Difference (APD) for measuring AoP calculation accuracy.To address these challenges, this study designed a keypoint detection model integrating a self-supervised encoder with a U-Net architecture [7]. Specifically, extensive unlabeled images were utilized for self-supervised pre-training to enhance the encoder's perception of structural features. Subsequently, fine tuning was performed on labeled images to train the network to generate precise heatmaps for locating the three key points. The maximum activation positions in the heatmaps were accurately mapped to original image coordinates through normalization and interpolation, enabling automated AoP calculation.This method demonstrated outstanding performance on the IUGC challenge test set, achieving ninth place among global participants, validating its stability and adaptability on real clinical images. These results not only showcase the application potential of self-supervised strategies in medical image keypoint detection tasks but also establish a technical foundation for promoting the clinical translation of intelligent obstetric ultrasound analysis tools.

2 Method

2.1 Method Design

The adopted network model is based on the classic U-Net architecture[11], comprising symmetrical encoder and decoder modules. The encoder consists of four convolutional blocks, each containing two consecutive convolutional layers equipped with batch normalization and ReLU activation functions, all using 3×3 convolutional kernels [6]. The spatial dimensions of the feature maps are progressively reduced through max-pooling layers while increasing the number of feature channels, enabling multi-scale feature extraction[5]. A bottleneck layer is incorporated at the deepest part of the network to further extract high-level semantic information.The decoder section employs transposed convolution (ConvTranspose2d) for upsampling, combined with feature maps from the corresponding encoder layers to achieve feature fusion and spatial resolution recovery. The final output layer uses a 1×1 convolution to map to the number of heatmap channels corresponding to the keypoints, with outputs normalized through a Sigmoid activation function[13].The model accepts three-channel color images as input and generates two-dimensional heatmaps for each keypoint as output, with the heatmap size fixed at 64×64. This network design maintains consistency with the self-supervised pre-trained encoder architecture to facilitate loading of pre-trained weights, thereby accelerating training and enhancing model performance. The model supports loading pre-trained encoder weights, importing only layer parameters with matching key names and compatible shapes to ensure parameter compatibility and initialization quality.

2.2 Model Architecture

A MoCo v2 framework was adopted to perform contrastive learning on large-scale unlabeled fetal ultrasound sequences. The encoder consisted of the customized U-Net encoder followed by a two-layer fully connected projection head. Input images underwent diverse augmentations, including random cropping and scaling, color jitter, grayscale conversion, Gaussian blur, and horizontal flipping. Positive pairs were generated from different augmented views of the same image, while negative samples were maintained in a feature queue updated by a momentum encoder. Training used a cross-entropy loss with the AdamW optimizer (learning rate $= 1e - 3$, weight decay $= 1e - 3$), a batch size of 64, and 200 epochs.

High-quality "gold standard" sequences [4] were identified by computing cosine similarity between candidate frames and a reference library using a ResNet50 feature extractor [9], with a threshold of 0.99. These sequences were then used to construct temporally adjacent frame pairs for further contrastive training under the MoCo v2 framework. Both query and key encoders were initialized from Stage 1, with the key encoder updated by momentum. A fixed-length negative sample queue of 16,384 was maintained. Training again used cross-entropy loss with AdamW (learning rate = 1e-4, weight decay = 1e-4, batch size = 64), along with a ReduceLROnPlateau scheduler. This process produced the fully fine-tuned encoder weights.

The fine-tuned encoder from Stage 2 was integrated into a U-Net backbone for supervised keypoint localization. Input images were resized to 256×256, and the network produced 64×64 keypoint heatmaps. Training employed MSE loss with the Adam optimizer (learning rate = 1e-5, batch size = 8) for up to 1000 epochs, incorporating early stopping and dynamic learning rate adjustment. A custom collate function was designed to filter out invalid samples. Experimental results demonstrated that two-stage self-supervised pre-training substantially enhanced feature representation and training stability, achieving lower keypoint localization[3] error and AoP prediction error compared to models without pre-training [?]. Ablation studies further validated the positive contribution of high-quality sequence screening and the phased self-supervised learning strategy to final model performance (Figs. 1 and 2).

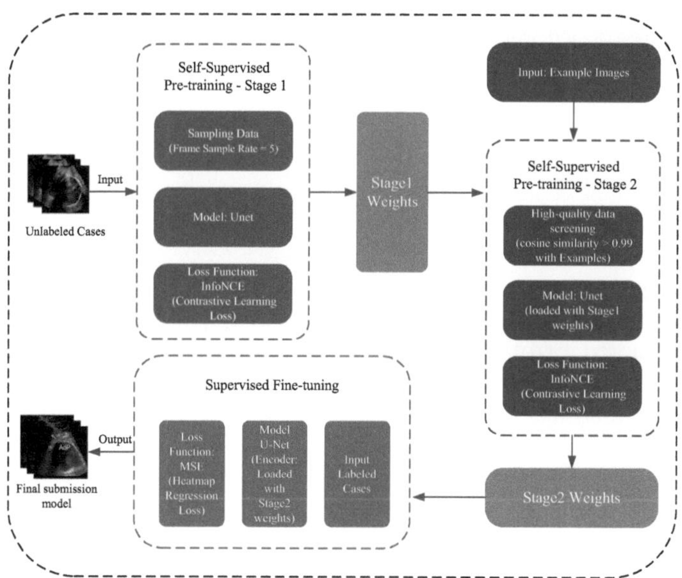

Fig. 1. This figure outlines the three-stage training pipeline of the proposed SSL-FetalBioNet model, which consists of two stages of self-supervised pre-training (MoCo v2) on unlabeled data to learn general feature representations, followed by a final supervised heatmap regression fine-tuning stage on labeled data for keypoint detection.

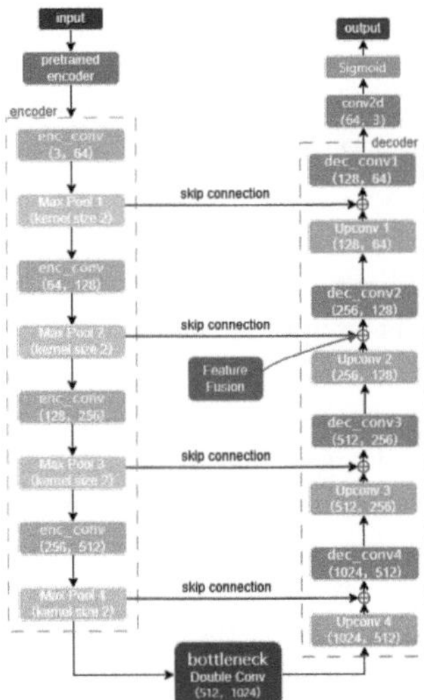

Fig. 2. This figure illustrates the core algorithmic architecture employed in our study. The model is based on the classic U-Net structure, where the left-side encoder pathway utilizes pre-trained weights for multi-scale feature extraction, while the right-side decoder pathway progressively restores spatial details through upsampling and feature fusion.

3   Experiments

3.1   Evaluation Metrics

This experiment selected four evaluation metrics to comprehensively assess the performance of the model in keypoint detection and AoP prediction, including Mean Squared Error (MSE), Mean Absolute Error (MAE), Average Point Distance, and the Mean Absolute Error for AoP (AOP_MAE). The specific definitions are as follows:

Mean Squared Error (MSE) is used to measure the squared difference between pixel values of the predicted heatmap and the ground truth heatmap. The calculation formula is:

$$\text{MSE} = \frac{1}{N} \sum_{i=1}^{N} (y_i - \hat{y}_i)^2$$

(1)

where y_i and $\hat{y}_i$ represent the true value and predicted value of the i-th pixel, respectively, and N is the total number of pixels.

Mean Absolute Error (MAE) measures the absolute difference between predicted values and true values. The calculation formula is:

$$\text{MAE} = \frac{1}{N} \sum_{i=1}^{N} |y_i - \hat{y}_i|$$

$$(2)$$

Average Point Distance is used to evaluate the accuracy of keypoint localization. It is defined as the average Euclidean distance between predicted keypoint coordinates and ground truth coordinates. The calculation formula is:

$$\text{Average Point Distance} = \frac{1}{K} \sum_{k=1}^{K} \sqrt{(x_k - \hat{x}_k)^2 + (y_k - \hat{y}_k)^2}$$

$$(3)$$

where K is the number of keypoints, and (x_k, y_k) and $(\hat{x}_k, \hat{y}_k)$ are the true and predicted coordinates of the k-th keypoint, respectively.

The Mean Absolute Error for AoP (AOP_MAE) quantifies the error in predicting the key angle parameter. The formula is:

$$\text{AOP\_MAE} = \frac{1}{M} \sum_{m=1}^{M} |a_m - \hat{a}_m|$$

$$(4)$$

where M is the number of predicted angle parameters, and a_m and $\hat{a}_m$ are the true and predicted values of the m-th angle, respectively.

3.2   Loss Function Analysis

In this task, the keypoint detection framework is based on a **heatmap regression** approach, which can be formalized as follows:

- **Target Heatmap Generation**: The ground-truth heatmap for each keypoint is constructed by centering a two-dimensional isotropic Gaussian distribution at the annotated coordinate location:

$$H_k(x, y) = \exp\left(-\frac{(x - x_k)^2 + (y - y_k)^2}{2\sigma^2}\right),$$

$$(1)$$

  where (x_k, y_k) represents the spatial coordinate of the k-th keypoint on the heatmap, and the standard deviation σ is set to 2.
- **Model Output**: The U-Net architecture predicts a corresponding heatmap $\hat{H}_k(x, y)$ for each keypoint. Each predicted heatmap is normalized to the range $[0, 1]$ via a sigmoid activation function.

- **Loss Function**: The discrepancy between the predicted heatmaps $\hat{H}_k$ and the target heatmaps H_k is quantified using the Mean Squared Error (MSE) loss, computed over all keypoints K and all spatial positions (H, W) within the heatmaps:

$$
\mathcal{L}_{\text{MSE}} = \frac{1}{K \cdot H \cdot W} \sum_{k=1}^{K} \sum_{y=1}^{H} \sum_{x=1}^{W} \left(\hat{H}_k(x,y) - H_k(x,y) \right)^2 . \tag{2}
$$

Here, K denotes the total number of keypoints, and $H \times W$ specifies the spatial dimensions of the heatmap (64×64 in this implementation).

This loss function enforces pixel-wise consistency between the predicted and target heatmaps, guiding the network to learn the underlying spatial probability distribution for each keypoint. The final keypoint coordinates are subsequently deduced by identifying the pixel locations associated with the maximum values (peaks) in the predicted heatmaps $\hat{H}_k(x,y)$.

3.3 Data Processing and Experimental Environment

In this study, the dataset provided by the IUGC Challenge was used, containing delivery ultrasound images with annotated keypoints and AoP parameters. To prepare the data for training, several preprocessing steps were applied. First, all images were uniformly resized from their original resolution to 256×256, ensuring consistency with the U-Net input requirements. The corresponding keypoint labels were then mapped to this resized coordinate system, and target heatmaps of 64×64 were generated using a Gaussian kernel to provide smooth supervision signals. In addition, pixel intensities were normalized to stabilize network training and improve convergence. The dataset was divided into training and validation subsets in an 8:2 ratio, with a batch size of 8. To handle potential issues such as missing images or corrupted labels, a custom filtering mechanism was integrated into the data loader to exclude invalid samples dynamically. These preprocessing operations–resizing, normalization, label transformation, heatmap generation, and data integrity checks–together established a robust and standardized input pipeline, providing a reliable foundation for supervised fine-tuning[12] and ensuring that the pre-trained encoder could be effectively leveraged for accurate keypoint localization and AoP prediction (Table 1).

3.4 Experimental Results

The experimental results indicate that when using ResNet as the baseline, all error metrics were relatively high. After introducing the U-Net architecture, which leverages skip connections to restore spatial details, metrics such as MSE and APD showed noticeable improvement. By further applying the complete training pipeline implemented in this study—including Gaussian heatmap supervision, MSE loss, dynamic learning rate scheduling, early stopping, and invalid

Table 1. Experimental environment configuration

System	Windows 11
CPU	Intel(R) Core(TM) i7-14650HX (2.20 GHz)
RAM	$16 \times 4GB/s$
GPU (number and type)	NVIDIA GeForce RTX 4060 16G
CUDA version	11.7
Programming language	Python 3.9
Deep learning framework	PyTorch (Torch 2.0.1)

sample filtering–significant performance gains were achieved even without loading self-supervised weights, reducing MSE to 343.8 and APD to 19.65. Building on this, the incorporation of two-stage self-supervised pre-training (combining MoCo v2 with golden sequence selection) further enhanced geometric localization performance, bringing APD and AOPMAE down to 18.90 and 6.97, respectively. This demonstrates that self-supervised learning effectively strengthens feature representation and spatial relationship modeling. Overall, the trend in results is highly consistent with the code implementation: architectural improvements lead to foundational gains, a stable training pipeline substantially reduces errors, and self-supervised pre-training further refines the accuracy of both keypoint localization and angle prediction (Table 2).

Table 2. Performance comparison of different methods

Model	MSE	MAE	APD	AOP_MAE
Resnet	626.9202	17.9708	28.7208	8.1679
Unet	571.4269	17.1102	27.6144	9.7752
U-Net w/o SSL	343.7685	**11.6983**	19.6536	7.5685
Ours (SSL-FetalBioNet)	**313.5583**	12.1833	**18.8999**	**6.9679**

4 Conclusion

In this keypoint detection task, our SSL-FetalBioNet model delivered strong performance on the validation set, achieving perfect detection (Missing Rate: 0.0000) across all 100 samples. The model attained a mean absolute error of 12.06 pixels and an average point distance of 18.73 pixels in localization tasks, while angular prediction achieved a mean absolute error of 7.00 degrees. Detection accuracy varied across anatomical structures, with errors of 11.37 pixels for PS1, 15.95 pixels for PS2, and 28.86 pixels for the tangency point. With an average inference time of 24.34 milliseconds per image, the proposed self-supervised U-Net framework demonstrates both efficiency and reliability in fetal ultrasound keypoint detection, showing particular strength in angle estimation and offering promising support for clinical biometric applications.

References

1. Aghasizade, M., Kiyoumarsioskouei, A., Hashemi, S., Torabinia, M., Caprio, A., Rashid, M., Xiang, Y., Rangwala, H., Ma, T., Lee, B., Wang, A., Sabuncu, M., Wong, S.C., Mosadegh, B.: A coordinate-regression-based deep learning model for catheter detection during structural heart interventions. Appl. Sci. **13**(13) (2023). https://doi.org/10.3390/app13137778, https://www.mdpi.com/2076-3417/13/13/7778
2. Bai, J., Khobo, I., Lu, Y., Ni, D., Yaqub, M., Lekadir, K., Ma, J., Li, S.: Landmark detection challenge for intrapartum ultrasound measurement meeting the actual clinical assessment of labor progress. Zenodo (2025). https://doi.org/10.5281/zenodo.15172238
3. Cano-Espinosa, C., González, G., Washko, G.R., Cazorla, M., Estépar, R.S.J.: Biomarker localization from deep learning regression networks. IEEE Trans. Med. Imaging **39**(6), 2121–2132 (2020). https://doi.org/10.1109/TMI.2020.2965486
4. Chen, X., Fan, H., Girshick, R., He, K.: Improved baselines with momentum contrastive learning. arXiv preprint arXiv:2003.04297 (2020)
5. Esteva, A., Chou, K., Yeung, S., Naik, N., Madani, A., Mottaghi, A., Liu, Y., Topol, E., Dean, J., Socher, R.: Deep learning-enabled medical computer vision. NPJ Digital Med. **4**(1), 5 (2021)
6. Hatamizadeh, A., Tang, Y., Nath, V., Yang, D., Myronenko, A., Landman, B., Roth, H.R., Xu, D.: Unetr: transformers for 3D medical image segmentation. In: Proceedings of the IEEE/CVF Winter Conference on Applications of Computer Vision, pp. 574–584 (2022)
7. He, K., Fan, H., Wu, Y., Xie, S., Girshick, R.: Momentum contrast for unsupervised visual representation learning. In: Proceedings of the IEEE/CVF Conference on Computer Vision and Pattern Recognition, pp. 9729–9738 (2020)
8. Litjens, G., Kooi, T., Bejnordi, B.E., Setio, A.A.A., Ciompi, F., Ghafoorian, M., Van Der Laak, J.A., Van Ginneken, B., Sánchez, C.I.: A survey on deep learning in medical image analysis. Med. Image Anal. **42**, 60–88 (2017)
9. Liu, Z., Lin, Y., Cao, Y., Hu, H., Wei, Y., Zhang, Z., Lin, S., Guo, B.: Swin transformer: hierarchical vision transformer using shifted windows. In: Proceedings of the IEEE/CVF International Conference on Computer Vision, pp. 10012–10022 (2021)
10. World Health Organization et al.: WHO recommendations on maternal and newborn care for a positive postnatal experience. World Health Organization (2022)
11. Ronneberger, O., Fischer, P., Brox, T.: U-net: convolutional networks for biomedical image segmentation. In: International Conference on Medical Image Computing and Computer-Assisted Intervention, pp. 234–241. Springer (2015)
12. Tajbakhsh, N., Jeyaseelan, L., Li, Q., Chiang, J.N., Wu, Z., Ding, X.: Embracing imperfect datasets: a review of deep learning solutions for medical image segmentation. Med. Image Anal. **63**, 101693 (2020)
13. Zhou, Z., Rahman Siddiquee, M.M., Tajbakhsh, N., Liang, J.: Unet++: a nested u-net architecture for medical image segmentation. In: International Workshop on Deep Learning in Medical Image Analysis, pp. 3–11. Springer (2018)

DSNT-DeepUNet: A Coordinate Prediction Method for Intrapartum Ultrasound

Zi Yang, Qingchen Liu, Yuchen Hu, Jingfan Kuang, Shanglin Song, and Jianlin Wang[✉]

The First Hospital of Lanzhou University, Lanzhou 730000, Gansu, China
448706606@qq.com

Abstract. Intrapartum ultrasound monitoring is critical for maternal-fetal safety, yet traditional manual annotation of key anatomical landmarks (PS1, PS2, FH1) faces bottlenecks such as significant inter-observer variability and time-intensive processes, hindering standardized implementation of the WHO Labor Care Guide (LCG). This study proposes DSNT-DeepUNet, a deep learning-based ultrasound coordinate prediction model. By integrating a U-Net backbone with a Differentiable Spatial to Numerical Transform (DSNT) layer, it achieves end-to-end mapping from raw ultrasound images to keypoint coordinates. The model employs a multi-task loss function to simultaneously optimize coordinate accuracy and heatmap distribution, while an 8-fold cross-validation strategy and dynamic data augmentation techniques significantly enhance generalization capability. On an independent test set, the model achieved an angle of progression prediction error of 4.7005 pixels and an average point distance error of 14.7712 pixels, with PS1 and PS2 localization errors at 9.0600 and 11.5661 pixels respectively, ranking sixth in a public challenge. This solution successfully eliminates subjective variations in manual annotation, demonstrating effective and precise ultrasound coordinate prediction.

Keywords: Intrapartum ultrasound monitoring · Anatomical landmark localization · DSNT network

1 Introduction

Intrapartum ultrasound examination, as a non-invasive and real-time fetal monitoring method, is widely used to assess fetal position, predict delivery methods, and aid clinical decision-making [9,11]. Studies have demonstrated its superiority over traditional digital vaginal examination in terms of objectivity, reproducibility, and patient compliance, significantly reducing discomfort and infection risks [6,11]. During the procedure, clinicians must manually annotate key anatomical landmarks—such as the symphysis pubis, the midpoint of the fetal cranium, and the umbilical cord insertion site—on ultrasound images to measure parameters like head-perineum distance (HPD) and angle of progression

J. Bai et al. (Eds.): IUGC 2025, LNCS 16317, pp. 33–46, 2026.
https://doi.org/10.1007/978-3-032-11616-1_4

(AOP), which are critical for evaluating fetal descent and predicting delivery outcomes [5,10]. However, due to subjective variations in operator experience, this annotation process exhibits significant inconsistency: multiple studies report an average localization deviation of 10–15 pixels for the same landmark across different clinicians, with a single annotation typically requiring 3–5 min [4]. Such limitations hinder rapid, precise monitoring in time-sensitive clinical settings, particularly during the second stage of labor where timely decision-making is crucial for avoiding adverse maternal and neonatal outcomes [5,9]. With the advancement of deep learning in medical imaging, automated keypoint detection via convolutional neural networks (CNNs) has emerged as a research focus, primarily following two approaches. First, direct coordinate regression uses fully connected layers at the network's terminus to predict coordinates [1,7]. While structurally simple, this method struggles to leverage spatial contextual information, limiting sub-pixel localization accuracy, and is highly sensitive to the spatial distribution of training data, which can hinder generalization. Second, heatmap-based methods generate probability distribution maps for anatomical points, with coordinates determined via non-differentiable argmax operations. Although preserving multi-scale features, this framework prevents end-to-end optimization (due to argmax's non-differentiability) and introduces quantization errors from limited heatmap resolution. To address these constraints, the Differentiable Spatial to Numerical Transform (DSNT) was proposed [7]. By computing spatial expectations over heatmaps, DSNT maintains spatial probability modeling while mapping discrete pixels to continuous coordinates, enabling gradient propagation and reducing quantization errors, all without introducing additional parameters [7]. Although DSNT has demonstrated superior performance in fields such as human pose estimation and facial keypoint detection [7], its application in medical ultrasound imaging remains in its nascent stages. Previous studies in medical imaging have largely relied on segmentation-based approaches, such as U-Net [8], for structure localization, which require pixel-level annotations and are time-consuming to produce [1,3]. Alternatively, regression-based methods that directly output coordinates have been explored to reduce annotation burden [1,3], yet they often lack the ability to provide spatial interpretability. Recent work has also shown that combining regression with implicit localization, as in biomarker regression networks [3], can yield both accurate measurements and spatial maps without segmentation labels, though such methods are still underexplored in ultrasound. This study utilized 300 cases of data provided by the competition organizers [2] and engaged three physicians with three years of experience in ultrasound diagnostics to annotate an additional 169 cases, resulting in a total of 469 intrapartum ultrasound datasets. For the first time, the DSNT module was seamlessly integrated into the heatmap branch of a deep U-Net, establishing an end-to-end differentiable localization framework. Building on this, the study designed a composite loss function that combines pixel-level Euclidean distance with heatmap distribution regularization, automatically optimizing their weights through grid search to balance coordinate accuracy and probability distribution quality. Furthermore, the study employed stratified 8-fold cross-validation and rigorous statistical testing to comprehensively evaluate model performance, with additional testing on a separate test set to validate the practical improvements in annotation efficiency and accuracy. The results demonstrate that the proposed method not only significantly reduces the average localization error of keypoints but also substantially shortens physicians' annotation time, offering a reliable and feasible technical solution for intelligent assisted analysis of intrapartum ultrasound.

2   Method Design

2.1   Methodology

The model architecture in this study adopts a deep symmetric dual-branch collaborative optimization framework, as illustrated in Fig. 1, to fully integrate multi-scale feature extraction with precise coordinate decoding capabilities. The heatmap generation branch employs an improved U-Net as its backbone network, featuring a seven-level progressive downsampling and symmetric upsampling design that enables hierarchical analysis from local textures to global anatomical structures. Specifically, the encoding phase utilizes 3×3 convolutional kernels with a stride of 2 for feature mapping during each downsampling step, followed by batch normalization and ReLU activation to effectively mitigate gradient vanishing and enhance the network's nonlinear representation capacity. As the network deepens, the number of channels progressively doubles from an initial 64 to 512, expanding the receptive field to capture anatomical information at varying scales. Concurrently, each encoder stage incorporates a 2×2 max-pooling operation at its endpoint to rapidly reduce feature map dimensions while preserving critical spatial information, ensuring computational efficiency.

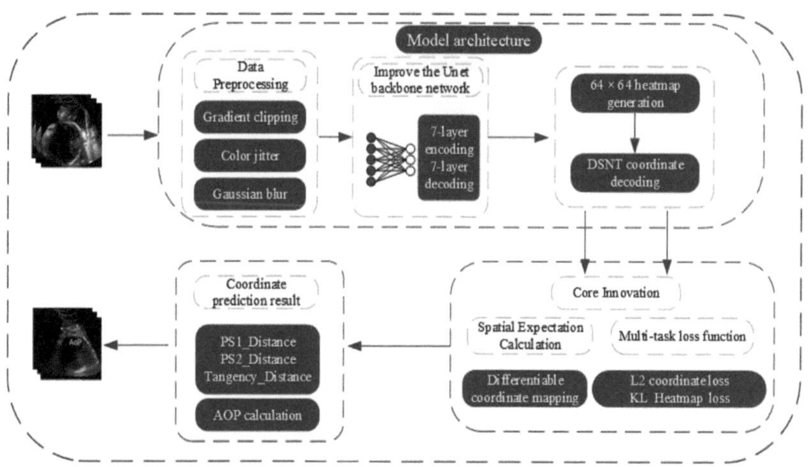

Fig. 1. Overall workflow

2.2   Network Architecture

The model architecture in this study adopts a deep symmetric dual-branch collaborative optimization framework, as shown in Fig. 2, to fully integrate multi-scale feature extraction with precise coordinate decoding capabilities. The heatmap generation branch employs an improved U-Net as its backbone network, featuring a seven-level progressive downsampling and symmetric upsampling design that enables hierarchical analysis from local textures to global anatomical structures. Specifically, the encoding phase utilizes 3×3 convolutional kernels with a stride of 2 for feature mapping during each downsampling step, followed by batch normalization and ReLU activation to effectively mitigate gradient vanishing and enhance the network's nonlinear representation capacity. As the network deepens, the number of channels progressively doubles from an initial 64 to 512, expanding the receptive field to capture anatomical information at varying scales. Concurrently, each encoder stage incorporates a 2×2 max-pooling operation at its endpoint to rapidly reduce feature map dimensions while preserving critical spatial information, ensuring computational efficiency.

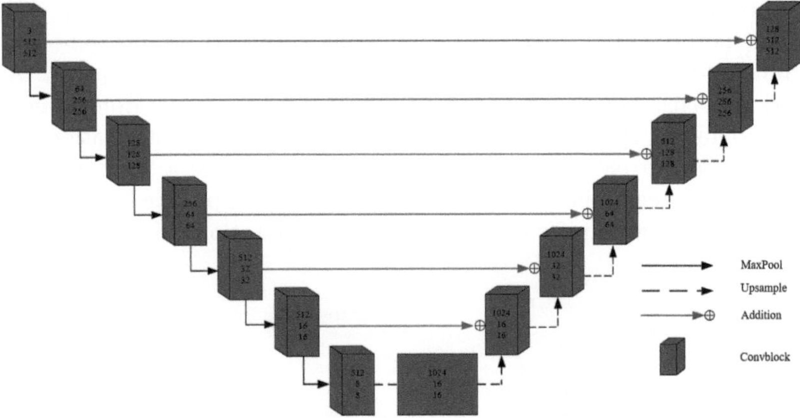

Fig. 2. Model Architecture Diagram

During the decoding phase, the model performs layer-wise upsampling via transposed convolution and smoothly restores spatial resolution through bilinear interpolation. Consistent with the traditional U-Net architecture, the decoder employs skip connections to fuse high-resolution features from the encoder at corresponding scales with the upsampled results, thereby mitigating the loss of deep semantic information. On this basis, the concatenated high-dimensional tensor undergoes further refinement through two consecutive 3×3 convolutional modules, effectively balancing spatial details with semantic integrity.

At the fourth decoding level, the 256-dimensional features extracted from the encoder's third level are concatenated with the upsampled 512-dimensional features, forming a 768-dimensional feature descriptor. This descriptor is then refined through successive convolutions to ensure that fused features at all levels adequately represent anatomical structural variations. Finally, the decoder output employs a 1×1 convolution to reduce the channel dimension to the number of keypoints (three channels in this study), generating a 64×64 heatmap where each channel corresponds to the probability distribution cloud of an anatomical landmark. This heatmap resolution, approximately one-eighth of the original image size, maintains sufficient spatial detail while keeping computational costs within a reasonable range.

The probability distribution maps generated by the heatmap branch are further fed into the DSNT (Differentiable Spatial to Numerical Transform) layer, enabling differentiable conversion from discrete probabilities to continuous coordinates. During model initialization, the DSNT module constructs and registers a Cartesian grid coordinate buffer with equidistant values in the range $[-1, 1]$, which is efficiently reused via tensor operations. In the forward pass, a pixel-wise Softmax is first applied to each heatmap channel to ensure the probability distribution adheres to normalization axioms. Subsequently, the expected coordinates of the keypoints are computed by performing an element-wise Hadamard product between the normalized probabilities and grid coordinates, followed by summation along the spatial dimensions. This mechanism fundamentally eliminates the quantization error inherent in traditional argmax operations and allows gradients to backpropagate directly from the coordinate loss layer to the heatmap generation branch, enabling fully end-to-end training.

In terms of model hyperparameter tuning, empirical optimization determined an optimal balance between a seven-level depth and 3×3 convolutional kernel size. The seven-level depth ensures sufficient receptive field coverage for complete anatomical structures while avoiding gradient vanishing issues associated with excessively deep networks. Fixed-size medium kernels enhance local feature representation while keeping parameter counts manageable. The channel doubling strategy draws inspiration from biological visual systems' multiscale processing, enabling the network to efficiently capture spatial details across different levels. The 64×64 heatmap resolution provides sufficiently fine-grained probability distributions for the DSNT layer while maintaining controllable GPU memory usage.

Overall, this dual-branch architecture forms a closed-loop optimization pipeline from 512×512-pixel ultrasound image inputs to three sets of keypoint pixel coordinates. The spatial features distilled by the heatmap branch not only encapsulate rich local and global information but also establish a differentiable coordinate learning pathway with the DSNT module. During training, the network optimizes both heatmap distribution quality and coordinate precision through a composite loss function, enabling the heatmap branch and DSNT layer to co-evolve and ultimately achieve sub-pixel localization accuracy. This framework provides an efficient, reliable, and easily deployable solution for automated annotation of intrapartum ultrasound images.

3   Experiments

3.1   Data and Preprocessing

This study constructed a dataset sourced from multiple Grade A tertiary hospitals and maternal and child health centers across China, including the First Affiliated Hospital of Jinan University, Zhujiang Hospital of Southern Medical University, Nanfang Hospital of Southern Medical University, the Third Affiliated Hospital of Sun Yat-sen University, Guangzhou Women and Children's Medical Center, and over ten other medical institutions, ensuring broad representativeness and clinical authenticity. The image data were acquired via transperineal ultrasound examinations using devices from various manufacturers, such as Philips CS50, Toshiba Aplio300, Voluson P8, Esaote MyLab, Mindray Resona series, and Youkey Q7, thereby ensuring diversity in imaging equipment.

Image acquisition was performed by an experienced specialized team, with all operators possessing more than seven years of expertise in ultrasound diagnostics. A standardized image acquisition protocol was followed, which included probe preparation, the application of coupling gel, and fine adjustments in positioning to ensure clear visualization of key pelvic and fetal anatomical landmarks while minimizing artifacts. Each case corresponds to a single ultrasound image. The training set consists of 300 images, and the validation set contains 100 images, making it one of the largest publicly available labeled intrapartum ultrasound datasets to date. Furthermore, three obstetricians from the First Hospital of Lanzhou University, each with over seven years of experience, independently annotated 169 ultrasound cases from an unlabeled dataset provided by the competition organizers. These data were also incorporated into the training set to enhance model performance.

To evaluate the model's robustness and generalization ability, an 8-fold stratified cross-validation approach was employed for dataset partitioning. Stratification was performed based on two dimensions–fetal presentation (cephalic, breech, transverse) and scanning laterality (left, right)–to maintain proportional distribution of different categories across all folds. Each fold was then alternately used as the validation set while the remaining seven folds served as the training set. This strategy not only maximized the utilization of limited clinical data but also ensured that each model evaluation covered diverse anatomical and scanning scenarios.

During preprocessing, to mitigate variations caused by different ultrasound devices and scanning parameters, all DICOM pixel values were first linearly normalized to the $[0, 1]$ range. Images with original resolutions ranging from 512×512 to 768×768 were resized proportionally using bilinear interpolation and center-cropped to a uniform 512×512 resolution to eliminate edge noise interference in model training. A PyTorch-based augmentation pipeline was applied to each image, including random color jitter (brightness, contrast, and saturation adjustments with an intensity of 0.4 each, and hue perturbation of 0.1), Gaussian blur, and a 50% probability of horizontal or vertical flipping. Additionally, random rotation (within $\pm 15°$) and translation (up to ± 10 pixels) were applied. All geometric and pixel-level transformations were synchronized with the original annotations via affine transformation matrices to ensure consistency between model inputs and target outputs.

To generate the target heatmaps for training, each ground truth keypoint was treated as the center of a 2D Gaussian distribution in the 64×64 low-resolution space. A continuous probability density map was then constructed within the [0,1] range, serving as the Gaussian target. These heatmaps, corresponding one-to-one with the network outputs, were used for subsequent regularization loss calculations, enabling the model to learn not only coordinate regression accuracy but also spatial consistency in probability distribution.

3.2   Evaluation Metrics

This experiment selects the following 4 evaluation metrics: Mean Squared Error (MSE), Mean Absolute Error (MAE), Average Point Distance (APD), and AOP_MAE.

Mean Squared Error (MSE): Quantifies the average squared difference between predicted and true values, emphasizing penalties for larger errors.

$$\mathrm{MSE} = \frac{1}{n} \sum_{i=1}^{n} (y_i - \hat{y}_i)^2$$

Mean Absolute Error (MAE): Measures the average absolute deviation between predicted and true values, more robust than MSE.

$$\mathrm{MAE} = \frac{1}{n} \sum_{i=1}^{n} |y_i - \hat{y}_i|$$

Average Point Distance (APD): Evaluates the average Euclidean distance between corresponding points in trajectory or spatial point prediction.

$$\mathrm{APD} = \frac{1}{n} \sum_{i=1}^{n} \sqrt{(x_i - \hat{x}_i)^2 + (y_i - \hat{y}_i)^2}$$

Error Metric for Anchor Offset Probability (AOP_MAE): Measures statistical error of bounding box offset in object detection or tracking.

$$\mathrm{AOP\_MAE} = \frac{1}{K} \sum_{k=1}^{K} \left| \mathrm{AOP}_{\mathrm{true}}^{(k)} - \mathrm{AOP}_{\mathrm{pred}}^{(k)} \right|$$

Additionally, we employed the Optuna hyperparameter optimization framework to systematically tune critical model parameters, including the learning rate, regularization factor λ, Gaussian heatmap standard deviation σ, and gradient clipping norm `clip_grad_norm`. The optimization objective was to minimize the combined validation loss $\ell = \ell_{euc} + \lambda \cdot \ell_{reg}$. After 50 trials, the optimal hyperparameter set was determined as: learning rate $= 5.352137134504593 \times 10^{-5}$, $\lambda = 3.732135829310275$, $\sigma = 2.30221666650613793$, and `clip_grad_norm` $= 0.7221588712934679$. This automated tuning process significantly enhanced model stability and convergence efficiency.

3.3 Experimental Environment and Configuration

This experiment was conducted on a Windows 11 Professional operating system. The hardware configuration consists of:

- NVIDIA GeForce RTX 4090 GPU with 24 GB VRAM
- Intel Core i9-13900K processor (24 cores, 32 threads, base frequency 3.00 GHz)
- 64 GB DDR5 RAM
- 2 TB NVMe SSD

The GPU's Tensor Core architecture and 24 GB VRAM provide powerful parallel computing capabilities for model training, while the processor's 24 physical cores efficiently support data preprocessing workflows.

The experiment is based on a PyTorch framework implementing the DSNT keypoint detection model. Parameter updates were performed using the Adam optimizer with an initial learning rate of 5.35×10^{-5}. During training, a dynamic learning rate scheduling strategy was employed: when the validation loss showed no improvement for 10 consecutive epochs, the learning rate decayed to 50% of its current value. This approach effectively balances convergence speed with training stability.

3.4 Loss Function Analysis

In deep learning keypoint detection tasks, the DSNT loss function achieves end-to-end coordinate regression through a dual-path supervision mechanism. Its core consists of Euclidean distance loss and probability distribution regularization loss, mathematically expressed as:

$$\ell = \ell_{\text{euc}} + \lambda \cdot \ell_{\text{reg}}$$

where λ is the tunable regularization factor (set to 3.73 in the code). The Euclidean loss directly constrains the normalized coordinate space: first, the true pixel coordinates are linearly transformed to the interval $[-1, 1]$, then the mean squared error between predicted coordinates and transformed true coordinates is calculated:

$$\ell_{\text{euc}} = \frac{1}{N} \sum_{i=1}^{N} \| \mathbf{C}_i - \mathbf{C}_{\text{gt},i}^{\text{norm}} \|^2$$

The regularization loss aligns the heatmap distribution via Kullback-Leibler (KL) divergence: based on true coordinates, a Gaussian target heatmap is generated where the heat value for each keypoint channel is determined by a 2D Gaussian function:

$$H_{\mathrm{gt}}(x, y) = \exp\left(-\frac{(x - x_c)^2 + (y - y_c)^2}{2(\sigma/\hbar)^2}\right)$$

This loss computes the logarithmic probability difference between the predicted heatmap $\hat{H}$ and the target heatmap:

$$\ell_{\mathrm{reg}} = \mathrm{KL}(H_{\mathrm{gt}} \| \hat{H}) = \frac{1}{NK} \sum_{i=1}^{N} \sum_{k=1}^{K} H_{\mathrm{gt}}^{(i,k)} \left(\log H_{\mathrm{gt}}^{(i,k)} - \log \hat{H}^{(i,k)}\right)$$

This dual-path design enables the model to simultaneously learn precise coordinate localization and heatmap representations conforming to spatial probability distributions, significantly enhancing regression stability.

4   Results and Analysis

4.1   Analysis of Loss and Pixel Error

In the eight-fold training, the seventh fold achieved the best performance. The analysis of loss and pixel error for the seventh fold is shown in the figure below (Fig. 3). Over the course of 66 training epochs, both the training loss and validation loss exhibited a consistent declining trend. The training loss decreased steadily from an initial value of approximately 1840 to around 1302, while the validation loss showed a similar downward trend, starting from about 1556 and eventually converging near 1364. This synchronous reduction in both losses indicates effective learning without signs of overfitting. The validation pixel error demonstrated significant improvement, dropping from nearly 20 pixels to below 10 pixels, reflecting enhanced localization accuracy of the model. It is worth noting that the learning rate was reduced twice during training (at epochs 44 and 58), which effectively contributed to the stabilization of the loss curves.

4.2   Analysis of Experimental Results

This study systematically evaluated the performance of three models on both validation and test sets, with the results shown in Table 1. The baseline U-Net model, an improved model with multi-scale fusion (Deep-UNet), and a model incorporating both multi-scale fusion and DSNT modules (DSNT-DeepUNet). The evaluation considered four key performance metrics: Mean Squared Error (MSE), Mean Absolute Error (MAE), Average Point Distance (APD), and Average Angular Deviation (AOP).

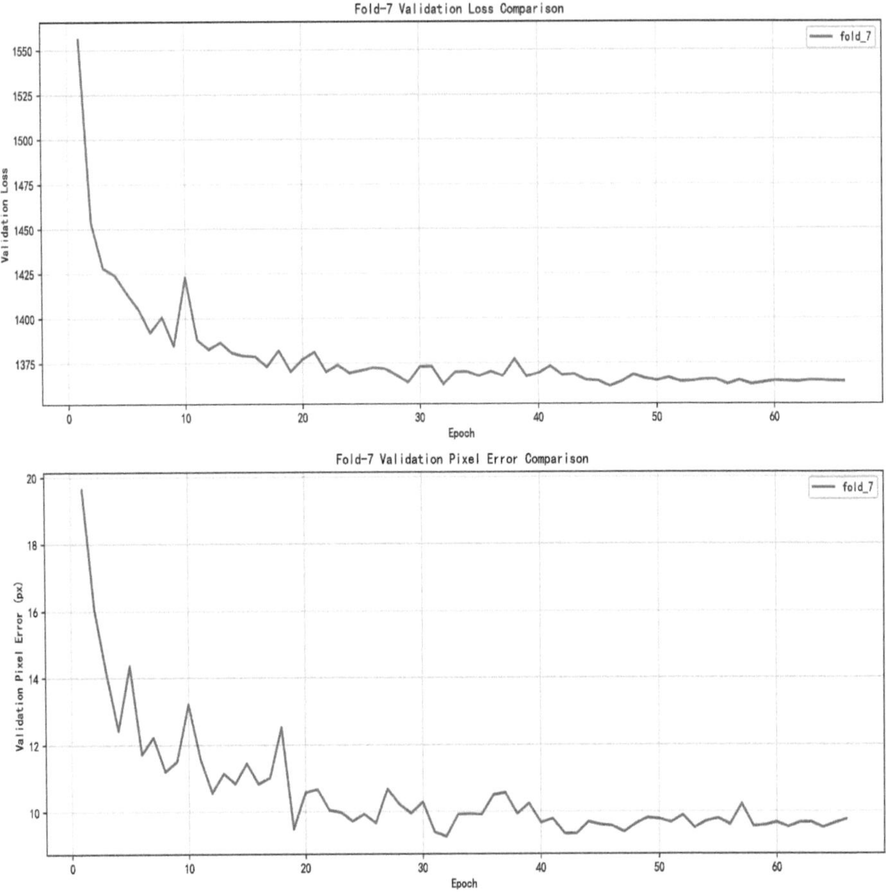

Fig. 3. Training and validation loss trends

Experimental results demonstrate that the DSNT-DeepUNet model, integrating multi-scale features and DSNT modules, achieved the best overall performance on both datasets. Specifically, on the validation set, DSNT-DeepUNet attained the lowest MSE (178.0195) and AOP (4.7906), with its MAE (9.9812) and APD (15.5995) outperforming the baseline U-Net (MSE: 632.6917, MAE: 13.0450, APD: 20.2612, AOP: 8.0364) while approaching or slightly trailing Deep-UNet (MSE: 219.8383, MAE: 9.9350, APD: 15.5393, AOP: 5.5850).

On the more challenging test set, DSNT-DeepUNet's advantages were more pronounced, achieving the best values across all four metrics: MSE (180.9396), MAE (9.4630), APD (14.7712), and AOP (4.7005). In comparison, Deep-UNet's performance on the test set (MSE: 273.8074, MAE: 9.8526, APD: 15.3954, AOP: 5.9237) remained significantly better than baseline U-Net (MSE: 887.5399, MAE: 14.0043, APD: 21.8273, AOP: 8.3727) but showed a comprehensive gap compared to DSNT-DeepUNet.

Overall, the multi-scale fusion strategy alone (Deep-UNet) effectively enhanced model performance, while the additional integration of DSNT modules (DSNT-DeepUNet) brought more substantial accuracy improvements. This was particularly evident in position (APD) and angular (AOP) prediction accuracy, ultimately establishing DSNT-DeepUNet as the top-performing model architecture in this study.

Table 1. Experimental Results

Dataset	Model	MSE	MAE	APD	AOP
Validation	Unet	632.6917	13.0450	20.2612	8.0364
Validation	Deep-UNet	219.8383	**9.9350**	**15.5393**	5.5850
Validation	DSNT-DeepUNet	**178.0195**	9.9812	15.5995	**4.7906**
Test	Unet	887.5399	14.0043	21.8273	8.3727
Test	Deep-UNet	273.8074	9.8526	15.3954	5.9237
Test	DSNT-DeepUNet	**180.9396**	**9.4630**	**14.7712**	**4.7005**

5   Model Tooling

Our team has operationalized the model described in the paper and developed a real-time automated tool for predicting the Angle of Progression (AoP) from intrapartum ultrasound images. When a single ultrasound frame is uploaded, the system automatically detects and precisely annotates three key anatomical landmarks–the two endpoints of the pubic symphysis (PS1, PS2) and the fetal head point (FH1)–within a standardized 512×512-pixel image coordinate system, and computes the AoP from these spatial coordinates. The system also generates a visualization showing the annotated landmarks, the connecting lines, and the angle markers, and returns this visual output together with the numerical AoP result instantly. This end-to-end, fully automated pipeline eliminates manual intervention, substantially shortens processing time, and reduces annotation variability, thereby providing an efficient and consistent method for clinical assessment of fetal head progression. The web link is: http://61.178.78.27:50210/aop_prediction/, as illustrated in Fig. 4.

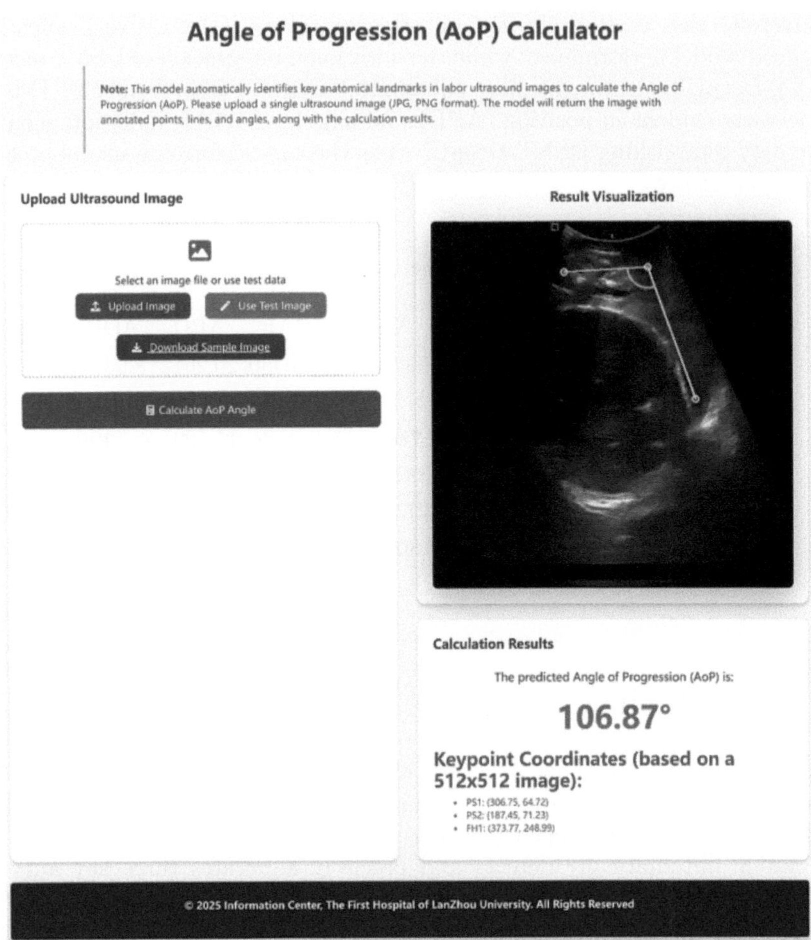

Fig. 4. Model Tooling

6 Conclusion

This study addresses the challenges of significant inter-observer variability and time-consuming manual annotation of key anatomical landmarks in intrapartum ultrasound monitoring by proposing a deep learning-based coordinate prediction model named DSNT-DeepUNet. The model integrates a deep U-Net backbone with a Differentiable Spatial to Numerical Transform (DSNT) module, achieving end-to-end mapping from raw ultrasound images to keypoint coordinates. This approach effectively mitigates quantization errors and non-differentiability issues inherent in traditional methods, significantly improving localization accuracy and inference efficiency.

By incorporating a multi-task loss function, the model optimizes coordinate prediction accuracy while enhancing regularization constraints on the heatmap probability distribution, thereby striking a balance between spatial consistency and numerical regression stability. An eight-fold stratified cross-validation strategy and dynamic data augmentation methods were employed, substantially improving the model's generalization capability and robustness. Experimental results demonstrate that DSNT-DeepUNet outperforms both the baseline U-Net and the Deep-UNet model with only multi-scale fusion modules on an independent test set, particularly in reducing keypoint distance errors and improving the prediction accuracy of the angle of progression (AoP).

Furthermore, the model has been operationalized into a web-based system capable of real-time ultrasound image processing and automatic AoP calculation, providing a consistent, efficient, and non-invasive auxiliary tool for clinical practice. The system is publicly accessible for testing and demonstrates considerable potential for clinical application.

Although the proposed model achieved sixth place in the open challenge with no missed detections, indicating high reliability, it still exhibits certain errors when handling complex anatomical structures such as tangent points. Future work will focus on optimizing the model architecture through the incorporation of attention mechanisms and multi-modal information to improve recognition capability for challenging cases, while expanding the dataset to enhance generalization across diverse devices and populations.

Acknowledgments. The authors of this paper declare that the method implemented for participation in the Landmark Detection Challenge for Intrapartum Ultrasound Measurement (Intrapartum Ultrasound Grand Challenge 2025) did not employ any pre-trained models or external datasets beyond those provided by the organizers. We extend our gratitude to all data contributors for making the ultrasound images publicly accessible.

This work was supported by the Education Development Foundation of Lanzhou University.

References

1. Aghasizade, M., et al.: A coordinate-regression-based deep learning model for catheter detection during structural heart interventions. Appl. Sci. **13**, 7778 (2023). https://doi.org/10.3390/app13137778
2. Bai, J., et al.: Landmark detection challenge for intrapartum ultrasound measurement meeting the actual clinical assessment of labor progress. In: Medical Image Computing and Computer Assisted Intervention 2025 (MICCAI) (2025). https://doi.org/10.5281/zenodo.15081529
3. Cano-Espinosa, C., González, G., Washko, G.R., Cazorla, M., Estépar, R.S.J.: Biomarker localization from deep learning regression networks. IEEE Trans. Med. Imaging **39**(6), 2121–2132 (2020). https://doi.org/10.1109/TMI.2020.2965486
4. Hu, N.N., He, Y.F.: Application value of ultrasound in labor. Chin. J. Clin. Res. **35**(05), 721–725 (2022). https://doi.org/10.13429/j.cnki.cjcr.2022.05.027

5. Huo, G.G., Chang, Y., Chen, X.: Value of transperineal ultrasound measurement of angle of progression and head-perineum distance in predicting delivery mode and duration in the second stage of labor. Chin. J. Pract. Gynecol. Obstet. **37**(03), 373–377 (2021). https://doi.org/10.19538/j.fk2021030123

6. Li, P.M., Wu, Z.M., Yao, L.M.: Effects of intrapartum ultrasound monitoring of fetal heart rate and fetal position combined with new labor stage time limit management on labor process and pregnancy outcome in advanced age parturients. Med. Innov. China **20**(21), 147–152 (2023)

7. Nibali, A., He, Z., Morgan, S., Prendergast, L.: Numerical coordinate regression with convolutional neural networks. arXiv preprint (2018)

8. Ronneberger, O., Fischer, P., Brox, T.: U-Net: convolutional networks for biomedical image segmentation. In: MICCAI (2015)

9. Yang, J.: Clinical study on the evaluation of delivery mode by intrapartum ultrasound combined with vaginal examination. Guide China Med. **22**(09), 55–58 (2024). https://doi.org/10.15912/j.issn.1671-8194.2024.09.016

10. Yue, Z.Z., Wang, J.Y., Ni, Y., et al.: Predictive value of transperineal ultrasound measurement of angle of progression and head-perineum distance in the second stage of labor for delivery mode and duration. J. Clin. Exp. Med. **21**(11), 1196–1200 (2022)

11. Zhang, Q.J., Yan, J.Y.: Application of intrapartum ultrasound in labor management. Chin. J. Pract. Gynecol. Obstet. **40**(02), 142–147 (2024). https://doi.org/10.19538/j.fk2024020104

Adversarially Fine-Tuned Self-supervised Framework for Automated Landmark Detection in Intrapartum Ultrasound

Anirvan Krishna[1(✉)] and Zaid Ahmed Khan[2]

[1] Department of Electrical Engineering, Indian Institute of Technology, Kharagpur, India
`anirvankrishna@kgpian.iitkgp.ac.in`
[2] Department of Chemical Engineering, Indian Institute of Technology, Kharagpur, India
`ik241168@kgpian.iitkgp.ac.in`

Abstract. Accurate assessment of fetal head progression during labor is essential for guiding timely clinical interventions and improving maternal-fetal outcomes. The World Health Organization's Labour Care Guide emphasizes standardized, evidence-based monitoring tools such as the Angle of Progression (AoP), derived from intrapartum ultrasound. However, current clinical practice relies on manual landmark annotation, which is labor-intensive and subject to variability. To address this limitation, we present a fully automated pipeline for anatomical landmark detection in intrapartum ultrasound as part of the Intrapartum Ultrasound Grand Challenge (IUGC) 2025. Our method combines (i) self-supervised pretraining on unlabeled standard plane ultrasound images to establish strong anatomical priors, (ii) an attention-enhanced decoder architecture for effective spatial localization, and (iii) adversarial fine-tuning using a PatchGAN-style discriminator to ensure anatomical plausibility and spatial precision. The model detects three key landmarks–two on the pubic symphysis and one on the fetal head–enabling robust AoP estimation. Our approach achieves a Mean Radial Error (MRE) of 25.66 pixels and an AoP Mean Absolute Error (MAE) of 8.54°. These results highlight the potential of self-supervised learning and adversarially guided strategies to reduce observer variability, standardize labor monitoring, and support global initiatives for safer, more equitable intrapartum care. Source code is available at https://github. com/VectorPoint-Analytics/IUGC2025.

Keywords: Adversarial Learning · Intrapartum Ultrasound · Landmark Detection · Self-Supervised Learning

1 Introduction

Effective intrapartum monitoring is critical for maternal and fetal outcomes. In 2018, the World Health Organization (WHO) issued 56 evidence-based recommendations for labor management, emphasizing timely and respectful care [1].

J. Bai et al. (Eds.): IUGC 2025, LNCS 16317, pp. 47–61, 2026.
https://doi.org/10.1007/978-3-032-11616-1_5

To implement these, the WHO introduced the Labour Care Guide (LCG) in 2020 to support real-time clinical decision-making [2]. A key element of the LCG is assessing fetal head progression, which influences decisions on operative delivery. Intrapartum ultrasound (US) has emerged as a valuable tool for this task, offering an objective and reproducible alternative to digital examinations. The International Society of Ultrasound in Obstetrics and Gynecology (ISUOG) now recommends ultrasound for labor monitoring [3,4]. Among quantitative ultrasound metrics, the *Angle of Progression* (AoP)–defined by three anatomical landmarks on standard plane (SP) intrapartum US (Fig. 1), namely the anterior endpoint of the pubic symphysis (PS1), the posterior endpoint of the pubic symphysis (PS2), and the fetal head (FH) [5]–is a widely adopted measure for assessing fetal descent. AoP correlates with delivery outcomes [6,7], but manual landmark annotation requires expert knowledge and suffers from inter-observer variability.

Angle of progression (AoP)

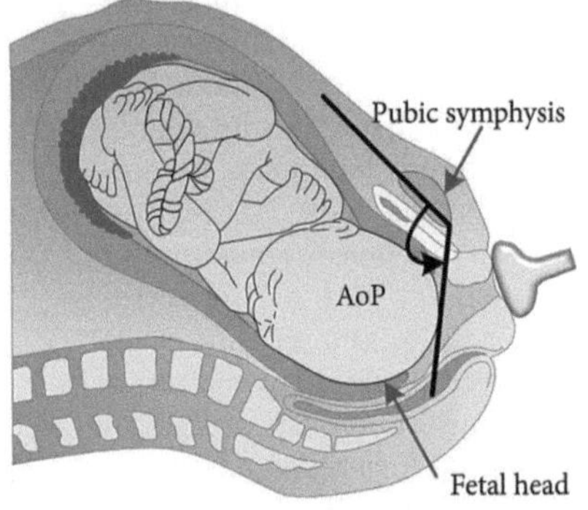

(a) Diagram of the fetus [8]

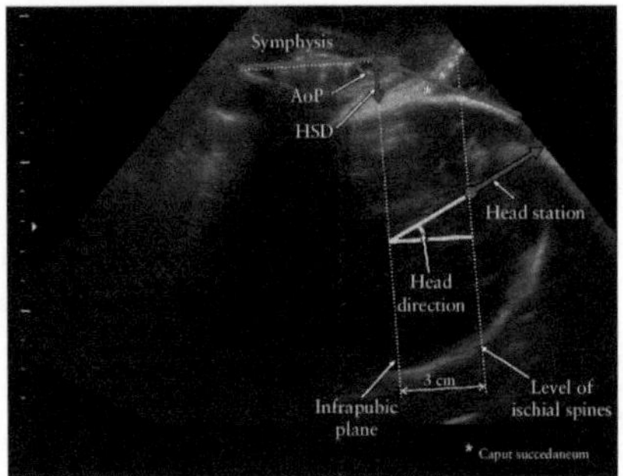

(b) AoP definition in Intrapartum Ultrasound [9]

Fig. 1. Description of Angle of Progression (AoP) defined using landmarks in transperineal intrapartum ultrasound on Pubic Symphysis (PS) and Fetal Head (FH)

Deep learning has demonstrated substantial potential in medical image analysis, including fetal biometry, placental assessment, and multi-organ segmentation [10–17]. While numerous studies have used ultrasound for fetal evaluation and anatomical measurements, its application to intrapartum ultrasound remains relatively underexplored. Existing works on Angle of Progression (AoP) estimation [12–17] predominantly rely on segmentation-based pipelines, which demand dense pixel-level annotations. Such annotations are costly, time-consuming, and challenging to scale, thereby limiting their utility in real-world labor ward settings. This gap highlights the need for scalable, label-efficient, and robust methods for AoP measurement.

To address the limitations of segmentation-based AoP estimation, our approach predicts anatomical landmarks directly from intrapartum ultrasound images, eliminating the need for dense manual annotations. This shift greatly reduces the annotation burden, enables more scalable deployment in diverse clinical settings, and maintains the spatial precision necessary for reliable AoP measurement. By leveraging unlabeled data and adopting adversarial learning strategies t enhance generalization in low-data regimes, our method offers a label-efficient and clinically aligned solution that supports standardized, evidence-based intrapartum monitoring in line with WHO's vision for improving maternal and fetal outcomes.

2   Methodology

Our proposed framework for automated landmark detection is composed of two primary stages: (1) self-supervised contrastive pretraining of a high-resolution encoder using the Momentum Contrast v2 (MoCoV2) framework, and (2) supervised fine-tuning of the encoder for heatmap-based landmark localization using adversarial guidance. An overview of the complete methodology is illustrated in Fig. 2, highlighting both the unsupervised representation learning phase and the subsequent supervised adaptation for landmark detection.

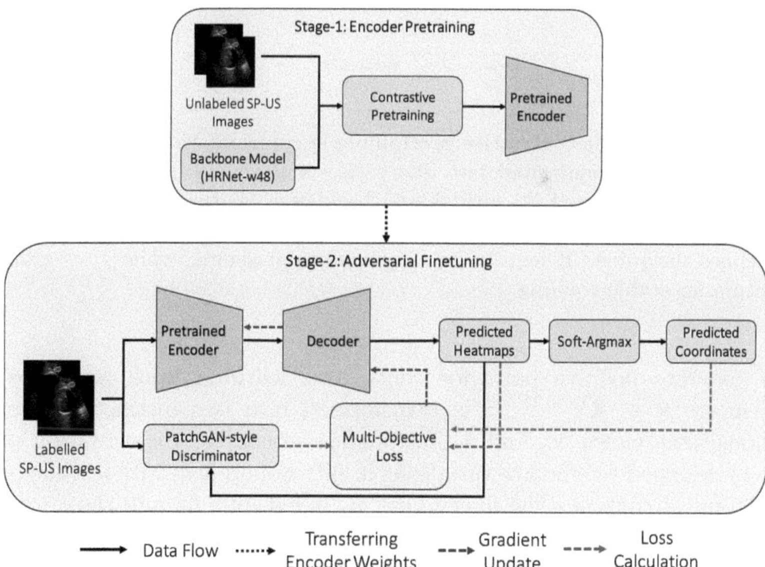

Fig. 2. Overview of the proposed framework. Stage 1: contrastive pretraining with MoCoV2 on unlabeled ultrasound images. Stage 2: supervised fine-tuning of the pretrained encoder for heatmap-based landmark detection with adversarial regularization

2.1   Contrastive Pretraining for Encoder

We employ the MoCoV2 framework [18] for self-supervised pretraining of a high-resolution encoder on unlabeled standard plane ultrasound images. An overview of the pretraining pipeline is shown in Fig. 3. In our setup, the backbone encoder is the High-Resolution Network (HRNet-W48) [19], chosen for its ability to preserve spatial resolution throughout feature extraction. The encoder described here is instantiated twice within MoCoV2: as a *query encoder* f_q and as a momentum-updated *key encoder* f_k. Both share the same HRNet-W48 architecture and initialization, but differ in their parameter update mechanism: f_q is updated via gradient descent, whereas f_k is updated via momentum tracking from f_q.

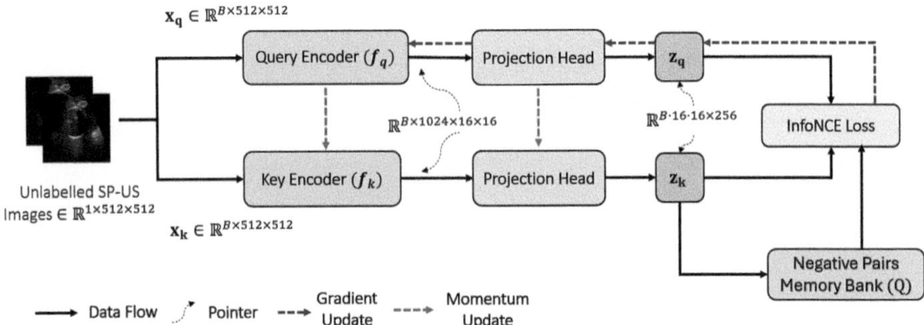

Fig. 3. Overview of the contrastive pretraining stage using MoCoV2. Each unlabeled ultrasound image is augmented into query ($\mathbf{x}_q$) and key ($\mathbf{x}_k$) views, encoded by f_q and a momentum-updated f_k with shared backbone. Feature maps are projected to embeddings ($\mathbf{z}_q$, $\mathbf{z}_k$) via a two-layer head. A queue of negatives with positive query–key pairs defines the InfoNCE loss 4. Only f_q receives gradients, while f_k is updated by momentum for stable training

To generate positive pairs for contrastive learning, each grayscale ultrasound image $\mathbf{x} \in \mathbb{R}^{1 \times 512 \times 512}$ is transformed into two distinct but semantically consistent views, $\mathbf{x}_q$ and $\mathbf{x}_k$, through a stochastic augmentation pipeline (Table 1) designed to emulate variations in ultrasound acquisition while preserving anatomical content. The query view $\mathbf{x}_q$ is fed into f_q, and the key view $\mathbf{x}_k$ into f_k.

Each grayscale ultrasound input $\mathbf{x} \in \mathbb{R}^{1 \times 512 \times 512}$ is first processed by either f_q or f_k, yielding a spatial feature map $\mathbf{f} \in \mathbb{R}^{1024 \times 16 \times 16}$. This feature map is then passed through a projection head, denoted as `ProjHead(·)`, which is configured as follows:

$$\texttt{ProjHead}(\,\cdot\,) : \texttt{Conv2D(256c1w0p1s)} \rightarrow \texttt{ReLU}$$
$$\rightarrow \texttt{Conv2D(128c1w0p1s)}. \tag{1}$$

The resulting output is a projected representation

$$\mathbf{z} = \texttt{ProjHead}(\mathbf{f}) \in \mathbb{R}^{128 \times 16 \times 16}. \tag{2}$$

Here, the shorthand notation $\texttt{XcYwZpWs}$ specifies convolutional layer parameters: $\texttt{c}$ denotes the number of output channels (X), $\texttt{w}$ the kernel size $(Y \times Y)$, $\texttt{p}$ the padding size $(Z$ pixels), and $\texttt{s}$ the stride length (W). For instance, $\texttt{256c1w0p1s}$ indicates a convolutional layer with 256 output channels, a 1×1 kernel, zero padding, and stride equal to 1.

Applying this projection head to the query encoder features produces $\mathbf{z}_q$, while applying it to the key encoder features produces $\mathbf{z}_k$. Each is ℓ_2-normalized across the channel dimension, after which the spatial dimensions are flattened to obtain:

$$\mathbf{z}_{\text{flat}} \in \mathbb{R}^{N \times 128}, \quad N = B \cdot 16 \cdot 16, \tag{3}$$

where B is the batch size.

MoCoV2 maintains a first-in-first-out (FIFO) memory bank $\mathcal{Q} \in \mathbb{R}^{128 \times K}$ of size $K = 8192$, which stores ℓ_2-normalized key features from previous mini-batches. This provides a large and consistent set of negative examples for the InfoNCE loss [20] defined as:

$$\mathcal{L}_{\text{MoCo}} = -\log \frac{\exp\left(\mathbf{z}_q^\top \mathbf{z}_k / \tau\right)}{\exp\left(\mathbf{z}_q^\top \mathbf{z}_k / \tau\right) + \sum_{i=1}^{K} \exp\left(\mathbf{z}_q^\top \mathbf{z}_i^- / \tau\right)}, \tag{4}$$

where $\tau = 0.2$ is the temperature parameter and $\{\mathbf{z}_i^-\}_{i=1}^{K}$ are negative feature vectors from $\mathcal{Q}$.

The parameters θ_q and θ_k denote the weights of the query and key encoders, respectively. While θ_q is trainable via backpropagation, θ_k is updated by momentum-based weight tracking:

$$\theta_k \leftarrow m\,\theta_k + (1 - m)\,\theta_q, \tag{5}$$

with momentum coefficient $m = 0.999$. This design stabilizes the contrastive objective by preventing rapid drift between the two encoders.

This spatially dense contrastive learning approach enables the encoder to learn rich local anatomical representations without requiring manual labels.

2.2   Heatmap Regression with Adversarial Supervision

Decoder Architecture. After pretraining, the HRNet-W48 encoder is fine-tuned for landmark detection by attaching a decoder head that transforms compact spatial features into high-resolution heatmaps. The decoder adopts a hierarchical design, wherein the encoded representation $\mathbf{f} \in \mathbb{R}^{1024 \times 16 \times 16}$ is progressively upsampled and refined through alternating convolutional and attention-enhanced blocks.

The architecture consists of composite attention-enhanced blocks ($\texttt{ConvCBAM2D}$). Specifically, each $\texttt{ConvCBAM2D}$ unit comprises a 2D convolutional layer (`Conv2D`), batch normalization, ReLU activation, and a Convolutional Block Attention Module (CBAM) [21], which jointly refines spatial and channel-wise feature representations. Formally:

$$\texttt{ConvCBAM2D}(\,\cdot\,) \mapsto (1\!:\ \texttt{Conv2D}) \rightarrow (2\!:\ \texttt{BatchNorm2D})$$
$$\rightarrow (3\!:\ \texttt{ReLU}) \rightarrow (4\!:\ \texttt{CBAM}) \tag{6}$$

The complete decoder $\mathbf{net}_{\text{dec}}(\cdot) : \mathbb{R}^{1024 \times 16 \times 16} \mapsto \mathbb{R}^{3 \times 512 \times 512}$ is defined as:

$$\mathbf{net}_{\text{dec}}(\cdot) \mapsto (1\!:\ \texttt{ConvCBAM2D})\,512\texttt{c3w1p1s} \rightarrow (2\!:\ \texttt{Upsample})$$
$$\rightarrow (3\!:\ \texttt{ConvCBAM2D})\,256\texttt{c3w1p1s} \rightarrow (4\!:\ \texttt{Upsample})$$
$$\rightarrow (5\!:\ \texttt{ConvCBAM2D})\,128\texttt{c3w1p1s} \rightarrow (6\!:\ \texttt{Upsample})$$
$$\rightarrow (7\!:\ \texttt{ConvCBAM2D})\,64\texttt{c3w1p1s} \rightarrow (8\!:\ \texttt{Upsample}) \tag{7}$$
$$\rightarrow (9\!:\ \texttt{ConvCBAM2D})\,32\texttt{c3w1p1s} \rightarrow (10\!:\ \texttt{Upsample})$$
$$\rightarrow (11\!:\ \texttt{Conv2D})\,3\texttt{c1w0p0s}$$

Here, each `Upsample` operation performs bilinear interpolation with scale factor 2 to progressively recover spatial resolution. This attention-guided hierarchical decoding ensures preservation of fine anatomical details, resulting in spatially precise and anatomically consistent heatmaps essential for downstream localization.

The final decoder output $\mathbf{H} \in \mathbb{R}^{3 \times 512 \times 512}$ contains a predicted heatmap for each anatomical landmark. Here, the spatial coordinates are denoted by $x \in \{1, \ldots, W\}$ (horizontal axis) and $y \in \{1, \ldots, H\}$ (vertical axis), where W and H correspond to the heatmap width and height, respectively. Landmark coordinates are estimated by applying the differentiable soft-argmax function [22] over each heatmap:

$$\hat{\mathbf{y}}_i = \sum_{x=1}^{W} \sum_{y=1}^{H} \mathbf{H}_i(x,y) \cdot [x, y], \quad \text{for } i = 1, 2, 3, \tag{8}$$

yielding final landmark predictions $\hat{\mathbf{y}} \in \mathbb{R}^{3 \times 2}$.

Discriminator Architecture. To enforce anatomical plausibility in predicted landmark heatmaps, we incorporated a spectral-normalized PatchGAN discriminator [23], denoted $\mathcal{D}$. It receives a predicted heatmap tensor $\mathbf{H} \in \mathbb{R}^{3 \times 512 \times 512}$ and outputs a patch-wise realism score map $\mathbf{s} \in \mathbb{R}^{1 \times 62 \times 62}$.

Each convolutional block (`SpectralConv2D`) comprises a spectral-normalized 4×4 convolution followed by a leaky ReLU activation:

$$\texttt{SpectralConv2D}(\,\cdot\,) \mapsto (1\!:\ \texttt{Conv2D}) \rightarrow (2\!:\ \texttt{SpectralNorm})$$
$$\rightarrow (3\!:\ \texttt{LeakyReLU}) \tag{9}$$

The complete discriminator $\mathcal{D}(\cdot) : \mathbb{R}^{3 \times 512 \times 512} \mapsto \mathbb{R}^{1 \times 62 \times 62}$ is defined as:

$$\mathcal{D}(\cdot) \mapsto (1:\ \texttt{SpectralConv2D})\texttt{64c4w2p1s} \rightarrow (2:\ \texttt{SpectralConv2D})\texttt{128c4w2p1s}$$
$$\rightarrow (3:\ \texttt{SpectralConv2D})\texttt{256c4w2p1s} \rightarrow (4:\ \texttt{SpectralConv2D})\texttt{512c4w1p1s} \quad (10)$$
$$\rightarrow (5:\ \texttt{Conv2D})\texttt{1c4w1p1s}$$

Spectral normalization is applied to layers (1)–(4) only, stabilizing adversarial training as proposed by Miyato et al. [24].

The adversarial component of the training objective is based on the least squares GAN (LSGAN) formulation [25], which stabilizes training and encourages sharper outputs. The discriminator is trained to minimize:

$$\mathcal{L}_{\mathcal{D}} = \frac{1}{2}\mathbb{E}_{\mathbf{H}_{\mathrm{real}}}\left[(\mathcal{D}(\mathbf{H}_{\mathrm{real}}) - 1)^2\right] + \frac{1}{2}\mathbb{E}_{\mathbf{H}_{\mathrm{fake}}}\left[(\mathcal{D}(\mathbf{H}_{\mathrm{fake}}))^2\right], \quad (11)$$

where $\mathbf{H}_{\mathrm{real}}$ and $\mathbf{H}_{\mathrm{fake}}$ denote the ground truth and predicted heatmaps respectively. The generator (i.e., the landmark detection network) is trained with the adversarial loss:

$$\mathcal{L}_{\mathrm{GAN}} = \frac{1}{2}\mathbb{E}_{\mathbf{H}_{\mathrm{fake}}}\left[(\mathcal{D}(\mathbf{H}_{\mathrm{fake}}) - 1)^2\right]. \quad (12)$$

This architectural design – integrating spectral normalization, CBAM-based attention, and a PatchGAN structure – enables the discriminator to capture subtle anatomical inconsistencies, thereby providing fine-grained adversarial feedback that improves both the accuracy and realism of the predicted landmark heatmaps.

The proposed model is trained under a multi-objective framework, where the overall loss is a weighted sum of four complementary components: (1) a heatmap regression loss $\mathcal{L}_{\mathrm{heatmap}}$, (2) a coordinate regression loss $\mathcal{L}_{\mathrm{coord}}$, (3) an adversarial loss $\mathcal{L}_{\mathrm{GAN}}$, and (4) an entropy penalty $\mathcal{L}_{\mathrm{entropy}}$. *Heatmap Regression Loss.* The heatmap regression term enforces spatial alignment between predicted heatmaps $\mathbf{H} \in \mathbb{R}^{K \times H \times W}$ and Gaussian ground-truth heatmaps $\mathbf{H}^* \in \mathbb{R}^{K \times H \times W}$ via mean squared error (MSE):

$$\mathcal{L}_{\mathrm{heatmap}} = \frac{1}{KHW}\sum_{i=1}^{K}\sum_{x=1}^{W}\sum_{y=1}^{H}(\mathbf{H}_i(x,y) - \mathbf{H}_i^*(x,y))^2. \quad (13)$$

Where $\mathbf{H}_i$ and $\mathbf{H}_i^*$ are the ground truth and predicted heatmaps respectively. This loss guides the network to learn pixel-wise probability distributions centered on the correct landmark locations. By regressing to smooth Gaussian targets rather than binary masks, the model benefits from stable gradients and improved robustness to small spatial deviations.

Coordinate Regression Loss. While heatmap supervision captures spatial context, it may not fully penalize small but clinically significant displacements of predicted peaks. Therefore, we introduce a coordinate-level MSE loss that directly measures Euclidean distance between predicted coordinates $\hat{\mathbf{y}}_i$ (obtained as shown in Eq. 8) and their ground-truth $\mathbf{y}_i^*$:

$$\mathcal{L}_{\mathrm{coord}} = \frac{1}{K}\sum_{i=1}^{K}\|\hat{\mathbf{y}}_i - \mathbf{y}_i^*\|_2^2. \quad (14)$$

This complementary term enforces precise localization at the point level, mitigating cases where heatmaps are visually plausible yet slightly shifted, which could impact clinical measurements.

Adversarial Loss. To ensure anatomical plausibility of predicted heatmaps, we integrate an adversarial loss based on the least-squares GAN (LSGAN) formulation as mentioned in Eq. 12 This term constrains the spatial configuration of landmarks to resemble anatomically valid patterns observed in real data, reducing the risk of unrealistic arrangements even when pixel- or coordinate-level losses are minimized.

Entropy Penalty. Ambiguous or overly diffuse heatmaps hinder reliable landmark extraction. To promote confident and unimodal predictions, we compute the Shannon entropy [26] over the spatial softmax of each heatmap:

$$\mathbf{P}_i(x, y) = \frac{\exp(\mathbf{H}_i(x, y))}{\sum_{x',y'} \exp(\mathbf{H}_i(x', y'))}, \tag{15}$$

$$\mathcal{L}_{\text{entropy}} = -\frac{1}{K} \sum_{i=1}^{K} \sum_{x=1}^{W} \sum_{y=1}^{H} \mathbf{P}_i(x, y) \cdot \log \mathbf{P}_i(x, y). \tag{16}$$

Minimizing this term encourages sharp probability peaks at landmark locations while suppressing irrelevant responses, thereby improving confidence and reproducibility in landmark detection.

Each component addresses a distinct aspect of the landmark detection task, thereby ensuring that the learned representations are spatially accurate, anatomically consistent, and confidently localized. The total objective is defined as:

$$\mathcal{L}_{\text{total}} = \lambda_{\text{h}} \cdot \mathcal{L}_{\text{heatmap}} + \lambda_{\text{c}} \cdot \mathcal{L}_{\text{coord}} + \lambda_{\text{adv}} \cdot \mathcal{L}_{\text{GAN}} + \lambda_{\text{e}} \cdot \mathcal{L}_{\text{entropy}} \tag{17}$$

where $\lambda_{\text{h}}, \lambda_{\text{c}}, \lambda_{\text{adv}}$, and λ_{e} are scalar hyperparameters controlling the contribution of each term.

3 Experiments

3.1 Dataset Description

We employed the official dataset from the Intrapartum Ultrasound Grand Challenge (IUGC) 2025 [27], which is designed to support research on automated Angle of Progression (AoP) estimation from Transperineal Intrapartum Ultrasound (TUS) images. The dataset consists of 31,421 training images, 100 validation images, and 501 test images. Among the training images, 300 are fully annotated standard-plane images containing landmark coordinates and AoP measurements, while the remainder are unlabeled. Within the unlabeled set, 2045 images are identified as standard-plane images. All images are stored in RGB format with a spatial resolution of 512×512 pixels. The validation and test sets are withheld from participants, with performance evaluation carried out exclusively via the challenge server.

For the self-supervised pretraining stage, we used the 2045 unlabeled standard-plane images to train the encoder backbone with the aim of capturing domain-specific features of TUS, in accordance with the ISUOG guidelines [28] which state that accurate AoP measurement requires simultaneous visualization of the longitudinal sagittal plane of the pubic symphysis and the fetal head. To enhance robustness to variations in acquisition conditions and to simulate realistic ultrasound noise patterns, each image underwent a series of spatial and intensity-based augmentations, carefully picked to mimic the natural variations in ultrasound images. Spatial augmentation included elastic deformation with parameters $\alpha = 5$, $\sigma = 10$, and $\alpha_{\mathrm{affine}} = 10$. Intensity-based transformations included random brightness/contrast adjustment, Gaussian blurring with kernel sizes in the range $[3, 5]$, and multiplicative Gaussian speckle noise with mean 0.0 and standard deviation 0.01. Augmentations were applied with probabilities as detailed in Table 1. Following augmentation, images were normalized to zero mean and unit variance with respect to the original intensity range (mean = 0.0, standard deviation = 255.0) and converted into tensors.

Table 1. Data augmentation parameters and application probabilities

Augmentation	Parameters/Range	Probability
Elastic Transform	$\alpha = 5$, $\sigma = 10$, $\alpha_{\mathrm{affine}} = 10$	0.8
Random Brightness/Contrast	brightness limit: 0.2, contrast limit: 0.2	0.5
Gaussian Blur	Kernel size $\in [3, 5]$	0.5
Speckle Noise	$\mu = 0.0$, $\sigma = 0.01$	0.5
Normalization	$\mu = 0.0$, $\sigma = 255.0$	1.0

In the supervised fine-tuning stage, we used the 300 labeled standard-plane images, each containing annotations for three anatomical landmarks: the distal edge of the pubic symphysis (PS1), the proximal edge of the pubic symphysis (PS2), and the most distal point of the fetal head (FH). Each image was also accompanied by a scalar AoP value. For heatmap-based regression, each landmark coordinate (x_i, y_i) was converted into a Gaussian heatmap centered at its location, with a fixed standard deviation $\sigma = 5$ pixels. The ground-truth heatmap for the i-th landmark is defined as

$$H_i(x, y) = \exp\left(-\frac{(x - x_i)^2 + (y - y_i)^2}{2\sigma^2}\right), \tag{18}$$

where (x, y) denotes a pixel coordinate in the image plane. The same augmentations listed in Table 1 were applied to both the images and the corresponding landmark coordinates to ensure spatial consistency between the inputs and the labels. This approach promotes generalization to unseen ultrasound acquisitions while preserving clinically relevant spatial relationships, which might be lost in the deeper layers of the network in an end-to-end regression pipeline (Fig. 4).

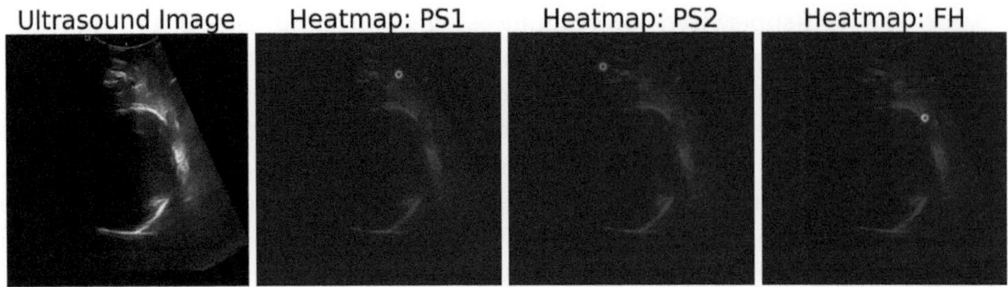

Fig. 4. Representation of the Gaussian heatmaps generated corresponding to the three landmarks present in standard plane intrapartum ultrasound image

3.2 Training Parameters

Self-supervised pretraining was performed for 25 epochs on unlabeled standard-plane ultrasound images with a batch size of 4. Feature projections were 128-dimensional, using a memory queue of 8,192, momentum coefficient 0.999, and temperature 0.2. Adam optimization [29] applied stage-wise learning rates to the HRNet-W48 backbone: 1×10^{-4} for the deepest stage, 0.5×10^{-4} for the intermediate stage, and 0.1×10^{-4} for the shallowest stage, with 1×10^{-3} for the projection head. Weight decay was 1×10^{-6}, and cosine annealing scheduling was applied over the total pretraining epochs. Mixed-precision training was employed.

Supervised fine-tuning was conducted for 400 epochs with a batch size of 4. AdamW optimization [30] was used for the generator (3×10^{-4}) and discriminator (5×10^{-5}), each with cosine annealing and weight decay 1×10^{-4}. The encoder was frozen initially and unfrozen in stages at epochs 150 and 250. The multi-objective loss (Eq. 17) is defined with weights $\lambda_h = 1$, $\lambda_c = 10$, $\lambda_{\mathrm{adv}} = 0.01$, and $\lambda_e = 0.001$. The choice of $\lambda_c \gg \lambda_h$ reflects the emphasis on precise landmark localization, while the small λ_{adv} stabilizes adversarial training without overpowering regression terms.

3.3 Evaluation

We systematically evaluated a range of encoder–decoder architectures, pretraining strategies, attention modules, and output representations for automated landmark detection and AoP estimation. Performance was assessed on the held-out test set using Mean Radial Error (MRE, in pixels) and AoP Mean Absolute Error (AOP MAE, in degrees) as evaluation metrics.

Mean Radial Error (MRE). The Mean Radial Error (MRE) is computed as the average Euclidean distance between the ground truth and predicted landmark coordinates:

$$\mathrm{MRE} = \frac{1}{3} \sum_{i=1}^{3} \sqrt{(x_i - \hat{x}_i)^2 + (y_i - \hat{y}_i)^2}. \tag{19}$$

This metric directly quantifies the pixel-level localization accuracy of the predicted landmarks. Where (x_i, y_i) and $(\hat{x}_i, \hat{y}_i)$ denote the ground-truth and predicted coordinates for the ith landmark.

AoP Mean Absolute Error (AoP MAE). The Angle of Progression (AoP) is geometrically derived from the three landmark coordinates (two endpoints of the pubic symphysis and the fetal head point). Let $\theta(\mathbf{y}), \theta(\hat{\mathbf{y}})$ denote the AoP values computed from the ground truth and predicted landmarks, respectively. The AoP Mean Absolute Error is then defined as

$$\text{AoP MAE} = \left|\left| \theta(\mathbf{y}) - \theta(\hat{\mathbf{y}}) \right|\right|. \tag{20}$$

This metric evaluates the clinical reliability of the method by measuring the angular discrepancy in degrees between the ground truth and predicted AoP.

4 Results and Discussion

The quantitative results for all encoder–decoder configurations are presented in Table 2. We systematically explored multiple combinations of (i) encoder architectures (HRNet-w48, ResNet-50 [31], and Attention UNet [32]), (ii) fully supervised vs self-supervised pretraining strategies (MoCoV2 and Masked Autoencoding), (iii) decoder designs with or without Convolutional Block Attention Module (CBAM), (iv) the use of adversarial regularization, and (v) output formats (heatmap regression versus coordinate regression). All models were subsequently fine-tuned on our dataset for landmark localization. Figure 5 illustrates the performance of the best model on representative training samples.

Baseline Performance. A fully supervised HRNet-w48 trained directly on the landmark detection task yielded an MRE of 43.88 px and an AoP MAE of 11.24°, reflecting the difficulty of the problem given the limited training data and the complex echogenic patterns in intrapartum ultrasound.

Effect of Self-supervised Pretraining and Attention. Replacing the randomly initialized encoder with a MoCoV2-pretrained HRNet-w48 and attaching a CBAM-enhanced decoder significantly improved localization accuracy (MRE 34.83 px), indicating that self-supervised pretraining effectively transfers domain-relevant spatial features and that CBAM helps focus on discriminative anatomical cues. Removing CBAM resulted in degraded accuracy (MRE 35.46 px), confirming the contribution of attention mechanisms.

Role of Adversarial Learning. Introducing a PatchGAN discriminator into the MoCoV2 + CBAM pipeline further reduced the error to 25.66 px (AoP MAE 8.54°), the best performance across all settings. This suggests that adversarial regularization encourages more anatomically consistent heatmaps, improving both localization and downstream AoP estimation.

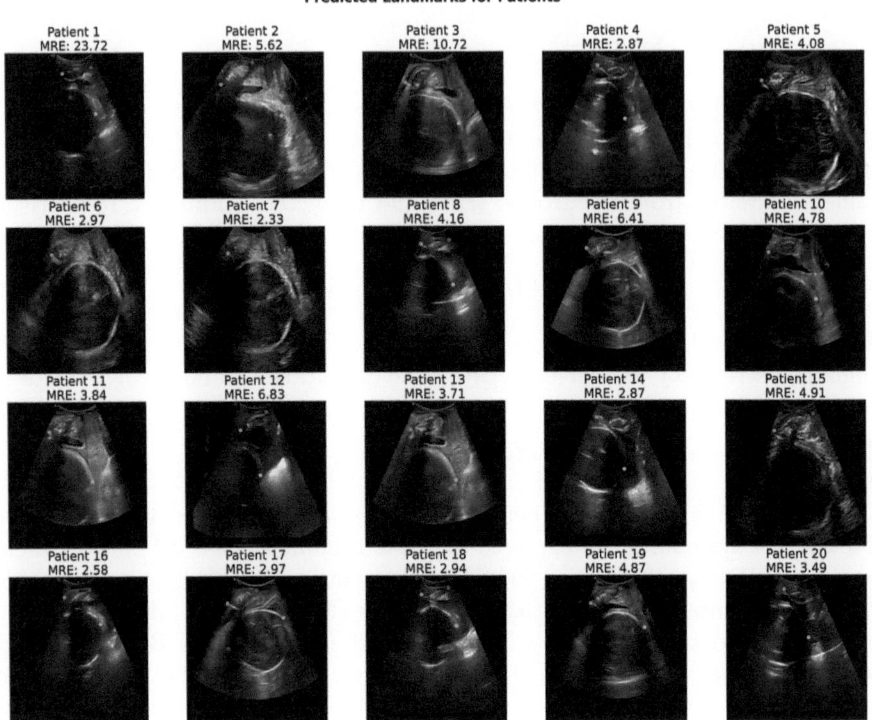

Fig. 5. Representation of landmark detection performance on 20 US image samples from the training set. The Mean Radial Error (MRE) is indicated for each of these images

Table 2. Performance of different encoder–decoder configurations, pretraining, attention, adversarial guidance, and output formats for landmark localization. Here, Attn denotes the presence of attention in decoder block, Adv. denotes the presence of adversarial guidance and AE stands for Autoencoder. The best scores are in **bold** and the second best are underlined. Downward arrow (↓) indicates lower values are better

Encoder	Pretrain	Attn	Adv.	Output	MRE (↓)	AoP MAE (↓)
HRNet-w48	–	–	–	Heatmaps	43.88	11.24
HRNet-w48	MoCoV2	✓	✓	Heatmaps	**25.66**	**8.54**
HRNet-w48	MoCoV2	✓	–	Heatmaps	34.83	12.26
HRNet-w48	MoCoV2	–	–	Heatmaps	35.46	13.85
ResNet-50	MoCoV2	–	–	Heatmaps	30.40	19.29
HRNet-w48	MoCoV2	✓	–	Coordinates	<u>29.64</u>	<u>10.68</u>
Attention UNet	Masked AE	✓	–	Coordinates	31.81	12.14

Coordinate Regression vs. Heatmap Regression. To assess the relative merits of coordinate prediction, we evaluated the same MoCoV2-pretrained HRNet-w48 + CBAM backbone with a coordinate regression head. This achieved an MRE of 29.64 px and AoP MAE of 10.68°, outperforming the fully supervised baseline and the heatmap-based counterpart.

These findings justify our *hybrid training objective*: combining heatmap regression with a differentiable coordinate extraction (soft-argmax) and an explicit coordinate MRE term. Heatmaps provide dense spatial supervision, capture uncertainty, and preserve contextual structure, while the coordinate term enforces geometric precision. The synergy of both was critical to achieving the optimal balance observed in our best-performing configuration in the adversarial setting.

Backbone Variation. Substituting the HRNet-w48 encoder with a ResNet-50 [31] (MoCoV2-pretrained) degraded AoP accuracy (MRE 30.40 px, AoP MAE 19.29°), highlighting the advantage of HRNet's high-resolution feature representations for fine-grained anatomical localization.

Masked Autoencoder Pretraining. A Masked Autoencoder [33] (MAE)-pretrained Attention U-Net [32] with a coordinate regression head achieved an MRE of 31.81 px and AoP MAE of 12.14°, outperforming the fully supervised baseline but not matching the MoCoV2-pretrained HRNet configurations. This suggests that instance-discrimination-based self-supervised learning may transfer more directly useful features for this task than masked image modeling in its current form.

5 Conclusion

In this work, we introduced a robust pipeline for automated detection of key anatomical landmarks–PS1, PS2, and FH–in intrapartum transperineal ultrasound images, enabling precise estimation of the Angle of Progression (AoP). Our approach integrates carefully designed models and training strategies to ensure strong generalization across diverse imaging conditions. By reducing reliance on manual measurement, the proposed method holds potential to enhance clinical efficiency, support objective decision-making during labor, and improve maternal–fetal outcomes. This work lays the foundation for future advancements in AI-driven intrapartum ultrasound analysis.

References

1. World Health Organization: Who recommendations: intrapartum care for a positive childbirth experience (2018)
2. World Health Organization: Labour care guide: user manual (2020)
3. Ghi, T., et al.: Intrapartum ultrasound: a review of current practice and challenges. Ultrasound Obstet. Gynecol. **52**(4), 437–444 (2018)

4. Ghi, T., et al.: ISUOG practice guidelines: intrapartum ultrasound. Ultrasound Obstet. Gynecol. **44**(4), 464–473 (2014)
5. Barbera, A.F., Pombar, X., Perugino, G., Lezotte, D.C., Hobbins, J.C.: A new method to assess fetal head descent in labor with transperineal ultrasound. Ultrasound Obstet. Gynecol. **33**(3), 313–319 (2009)
6. Ghi, T., et al.: Sonographic pattern of fetal head descent: relationship with duration of active second stage of labor and mode of delivery. Ultrasound Obstet. Gynecol. **44**(1), 82–89 (2014)
7. Barbera, A.F., Pombar, X., Hobbins, J.C., Melchor, J.C., Roque, C., D'Antonio, F.: Angle of progression: a valuable ultrasound parameter to predict operative delivery. Am. J. Obstet. Gynecol. **213**(2), 229.e1 (2015)
8. Yaosheng, L., et al.: Multitask deep neural network for the fully automatic measurement of the angle of progression. Comput. Math. Meth. Med. **1−14**(09), 2022 (2022)
9. Ghi, T., et al.: ISUOG practice guidelines: intrapartum ultrasound. Ultrasound Obstet. Gynecol. **52**, 128–139 (2018)
10. Barros, R.S., O'Connor, M., Noble, J.A.: Towards real-time angle of progression estimation from transperineal ultrasound using deep learning. In: Proceedings of the IEEE International Conference on Biomedical and Health Informatics (BHI), pp. 1–4 (2020)
11. Cerrolaza, J.J., Mukhopadhyay, A., Cerrolaza, N., Heinrich, M.P., Noble, J.A.: Weakly supervised learning of the angle of progression from transperineal ultrasound. IEEE Trans. Med. Imaging **41**(4), 802–814 (2022)
12. Zhu, Y., Singh, P., Vasudevan, S., Esfandiari, H., Noble, J.A.: Attention-based deep learning for landmark detection in intrapartum ultrasound. In: Proceedings of the International Conference on Medical Image Computing and Computer-Assisted Intervention (MICCAI). LNCS, vol. 14225, pp. 457–466. Springer (2023)
13. Long, S., Campello, V.M., Bai, J., Lekadir, K., Chen, Z., Lu, Y.: Fetal head and pubic symphysis segmentation in intrapartum ultrasound image using a dual-path boundary-guided residual network. IEEE J. Biomed. Health Inform. **28**(8), 4648–4659 (2024)
14. Zhou, M., et al.: Multitask deep neural network for the fully automatic measurement of the angle of progression. Comput. Math. Meth. Med. **2022**, 5192338 (2022)
15. Lu, Y.S., et al.: A framework for computing angle of progression from transperineal ultrasound images for evaluating fetal head descent using a novel double branch network. Front. Physiol. **13**, 940150 (2022)
16. Cai, P., Jiang, L., Li, Y., Lan, L.: Pubic symphysis-fetal head segmentation using pure transformer with bi-level routing attention (2024)
17. Zhou, Z., et al.: Segment anything model for fetal head-pubic symphysis segmentation in intrapartum ultrasound image analysis. Exp. Syst. Appl. **263**, 125699 (2025)
18. He, K., Fan, H., Wu, Y., Xie, S., Girshick, R.: Momentum contrast for unsupervised visual representation learning. In: Proceedings of the IEEE/CVF Conference on Computer Vision and Pattern Recognition (CVPR). pp. 9729–9738 (2020)
19. Sun, K., Xiao, B., Liu, D., Wang, J.: Deep high-resolution representation learning for visual recognition. In: Proceedings of the IEEE/CVF Conference on Computer Vision and Pattern Recognition (CVPR), pp. 5406–5415 (2019)
20. van den Oord, A., Li, Y., Vinyals, O.: Representation learning with contrastive predictive coding (2019)

21. Woo, S., Park, J., Lee, J.-Y., Kweon, I.S.: CBAM: convolutional block attention module. In: Proceedings of the European Conference on Computer Vision (ECCV), pp. 3–19 (2018)
22. Luvizon, D.C., Picard, D., Tabia, H.: Human pose regression by combining indirect part detection and contextual information. In: Computer Vision and Image Understanding, vol. 192, pp. 102897. Elsevier (2020)
23. Isola, P., Zhu, J.-Y., Zhou, T., Efros, A.A.: Image-to-image translation with conditional adversarial networks. In: Proceedings of the IEEE Conference on Computer Vision and Pattern Recognition (CVPR), pp. 1125–1134 (2017)
24. Miyato, T., Kataoka, T., Koyama, M., Yoshida, Y.: Spectral normalization for generative adversarial networks. In: International Conference on Learning Representations (ICLR) (2018)
25. Mao, X., Li, Q., Xie, H., Lau, R.Y.K., Wang, Z., Smolley, S.P.: Least squares generative adversarial networks. In: Proceedings of the IEEE International Conference on Computer Vision (ICCV), pp. 2794–2802 (2017)
26. Shannon, C.E.: A mathematical theory of communication. Bell Syst. Tech. J. **27**(3), 379–423 (1948)
27. Bai, J., et al.: Landmark detection challenge for intrapartum ultrasound measurement: meeting the actual clinical assessment of labor progress. Dataset, Version v1, Zenodo, March 2025
28. Ghi, T., et al.: ISUOG practice guidelines: intrapartum ultrasound. Ultrasound Obstet. Gynecol. **52**(1), 128–139 (2018)
29. Kingma, D.P., Ba, J.: Adam: a method for stochastic optimization. CoRR abs/1412.6980 (2014)
30. Loshchilov, I., Hutter, F.: Decoupled weight decay regularization (2019)
31. He, K., Zhang, X., Ren, S., Sun, J.: Deep residual learning for image recognition. In: Proceedings of the IEEE Conference on Computer Vision and Pattern Recognition (CVPR), pp. 770–778 (2016)
32. Oktay, O., et al.: Attention U-Net: learning where to look for the pancreas. arXiv preprint arXiv:1804.03999 (2018)
33. He, K., Chen, X., Xie, S., Li, Y., Dollar, P., Girshick, R.: Masked autoencoders are scalable vision learners. In: Proceedings of the IEEE/CVF Conference on Computer Vision and Pattern Recognition (CVPR), pp. 16000–16009 (2022)

Progressive Semi-supervised Landmark Detection Algorithm For Intrapartum Ultrasound Measurement

Zelan Li, Hansen Zhang, Zhengyang Zhang, Yan Cheng, Siqi Wang,
and Jianning Chi[✉]

Northeastern University, Shenyang, China
chijianning@mail.neu.edu.cn

Abstract. The angle of progression (AoP) in intrapartum ultrasound is critical for evaluating fetal head descent and rotation during labor, and the angle formed by these three points (PS1, PS2, and FH1). Manual AoP measurement is time-consuming, labor-intensive, and lacks standardization–limitations. However, automated methods encounter two significant challenges: firstly, the scarcity of landmark annotations provided by experienced obstetricians may lead to network overfitting and poor generalization; secondly, the anatomical landmarks in ultrasound images are often too small, resulting in insufficient information and feature learning for algorithms. To address these challenges, inspired by the clinical workflow of manual AoP assessment, we propose a progressive semi-supervised landmark detection algorithm, which first locates and identifies the pubic symphysis (PS) and the fetal head (FH) region, and then detects the landmarks of three keypoints to calculate the AoP. Specifically, in the first stage, we utilize the spatial information of landmarks to generate scribbles of the foreground and background of the PS and the FH region. These scribbles are fed to a frozen segmentation foundation model named ScribblePrompt to get coarse segmentation and detection results as pseudo labels, which can help the network concentrate on PS and FH regions. After the first stage of pseudo-label pretraining, the following fine-tuning utilizes pre-trained models to learn landmarks with confidence-guided weight loss to train on labeled and unlabeled data, improving the robustness and generalization of the algorithm. The experimental results show that our algorithm achieved good landmark detection results.

Keywords: Landmark detection · Semi-supervised learning · Intrapartum ultrasound.

1 Introduction

Labor is a dynamic process that requires continuous monitoring to ensure the safety of both mother and fetus [4,9]. A fundamental component of ultrasound-based intrapartum assessment lies in the accurate identification of anatomical

---

Zelan Li and Hansen Zhang—These authors contributed equally to this work.

© The Author(s), under exclusive license to Springer Nature Switzerland AG 2026
J. Bai et al. (Eds.): IUGC 2025, LNCS 16317, pp. 62–76, 2026.
https://doi.org/10.1007/978-3-032-11616-1_6

landmarks within intrapartum ultrasound images, as these landmarks serve as the basis for calculating critical clinical parameters such as the angle of progression (AoP) [7,23]. The AoP offers pivotal insights into fetal head descent and rotation during labor, and its measurement directly informs clinical decision-making regarding obstetric interventions. However, current clinical workflows rely on time-intensive manual landmark identification and AoP calculation by experienced obstetricians, and inherent intra- and inter-observer variability in these manual processes undermines the reliability and consistency of measurement results. In contrast, automated landmark detection algorithms for ultrasound images enable the rapid acquisition of standardized assessment outcomes, significantly reducing the time burden on clinical practitioners and thereby facilitating the efficient management of labor processes [3,13,28]. Consequently, an efficient and accurate automated ultrasound landmark detection algorithm holds substantial clinical application value [2,29].

Existing landmark detection approaches can be categorized into two paradigms: 1) Regression methods based on directly comparing landmark coordinates of prediction and landmarks. 2) Methods that treated landmark detection as a classification task based on landmark heatmaps, which typically transform the prediction of landmark locations into a heatmap classification problem. For instance, Sofka et al. [19] proposed a Fully Convolutional Neural Network (FCN) for the accurate automatic detection of measurement points in ultrasound video sequences, utilizing Long Short-Term Memory cells to ensure temporal consistency. YOLOv11 Pose [11] extends the original YOLO framework by integrating a keypoint detection module that enables simultaneous real-time object detection and human pose estimation, leveraging a single neural network to predict both bounding boxes and pose keypoints effectively. Alternatively, certain approaches [16,26] generate a Gaussian heatmap for each landmark and take the location with the maximum value as the ultimate prediction. However, these automated methods face two key challenges in intrapartum Ultrasound Measurement: 1) Landmark annotation relies on experienced obstetricians to manually label ultrasound images, a process that is both tedious and time-consuming. The scarcity of landmark annotations provided by experienced obstetricians can lead to network overfitting and poor generalization; 2) the anatomical landmarks in ultrasound images are often too small, providing limited information per point, resulting in insufficient information and feature learning for algorithms.

In this study, inspired by the clinical workflow of manual AoP assessment [1,12,14], we propose a progressive semi-supervised landmark detection algorithm based on the state-of-the-art YOLOv11 Pose framework for intrapartum ultrasound measurement. Adopting a coarse-to-fine strategy, the algorithm first locates and identifies the pubic symphysis (PS) and the fetal head (FH) region, and then detects the landmarks of three keypoints to calculate the AoP. In the first stage, spatial information of landmarks is leveraged to generate scribble annotations for the foreground and background regions corresponding to the pubic symphysis (PS) and fetal head (FH). These scribbles are input to a frozen segmentation foundation model, ScribblePrompt [24], to obtain coarse segmentation results and detection outputs as pseudo-labels, thereby guiding the network to focus on these critical anatomical regions [10,30]. Following the first-stage pseudo-label pre-training, the network incorporates anatomical priors, after which the second stage employs a confidence-weighted strategy for labeled and unlabeled data training to fine-tune the pre-trained model, yielding precise landmark detection results. Experimental findings demonstrate that the proposed algorithm achieves promising performance in landmark detection tasks. In summary, the contributions of our work are as follows:

1. We proposed a progressive learning strategy for intrapartum ultrasound measurement learning landmark from coarse to fine.
2. We proposed a scribble generation strategy based on prior anatomical structure, which extracts anatomical prior information of ultrasound images from landmarks, expanding prior knowledge from point range to region range.
3. We proposed a confidence-weighted learning strategy to utilize unlabeled images to enhance the generalization and robustness of the algorithm.

2   Method

Motivation. The main process for measuring the Angle of Progression (AoP) involves obstetricians first identifying the two farthest points (PS1 and PS2) along the contour of the pubic symphysis (PS) [5,6,17]. Then, a tangent line is drawn from the rightmost point (PS1) such that it just touches the fetal head (FH), with the intersection point marked as the third point (FH1). The AoP is defined as the angle formed by these three points (PS1, PS2, and FH1).

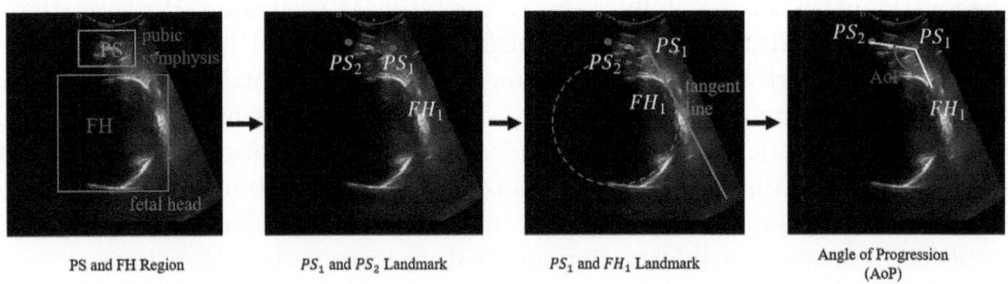

Fig. 1. The main process for measuring the Angle of Progression (AoP)

We observe that these landmarks are derived from the spatial relationships between distinct meaningful regions in ultrasound images, rather than from the direct features of individual points. However, in the task of the IUGC2025 challenge, the limited labeled data only provides the coordinates of PS1, PS2, and FH1. Since these three points are respectively located in two separate regions of interest (ROIs)–the pubic symphysis (PS) and the fetal head (FH)–it is not feasible to directly obtain the prior anatomical information of the PS and FH regions using only these landmarks. To address this limitation, we propose leveraging foundation models with high generalization ability to generate coarse region indications, thereby providing the network with the necessary prior anatomical information.

2.1 Overall Framework

As shown in Fig. 6, the proposed network progressively learns to detect coarse-to-fine landmarks in fetal ultrasound images for aortic pressure (Aop) measurement. The training process consists of two stages: In the first stage, we generate high-confidence scribbles based on anatomical spatial relationships as prompts for ScribblePrompt [24] to produce coarse segmentation results and the region of interest (ROI) pseudo-labels. In the second stage, the pre-training backbone network YOLOv11 is utilized to learn landmarks from labeled images and then generate pseudo labels for unlabeled images. The unlabeled images are used to help improve the generalization and robustness of the network through a confidence-weighted strategy.

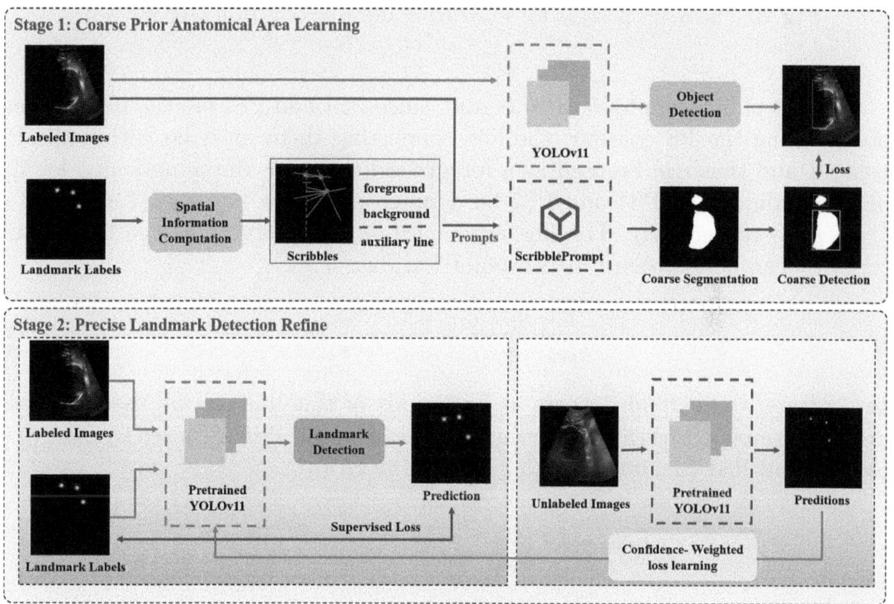

Fig. 2. Overall framework of proposed methods. In stage one, the network learns the coarse prior anatomical area through ScribblePrompt results, which prompted spatial information. In stage two, the network learns landmarks from labeled images and is further refined by unlabeled images with a confidence-weighted loss strategy.

2.2   Coarse Prior Anatomical Area Learning

Generation of Scribble Prompts. The ScribblePrompt [24] proposed by Hallee E. Wong et al. is a flexible neural network-based interactive segmentation tool for biomedical imaging. It allows human annotators to segment previously unseen structures using scribbles [15]. Therefore, we propose a method of spatial information computation: by extracting the spatial relationships between labeled coordinates and ROI regions, we generate scribbles that serve as prompts for input into ScribblePrompt.

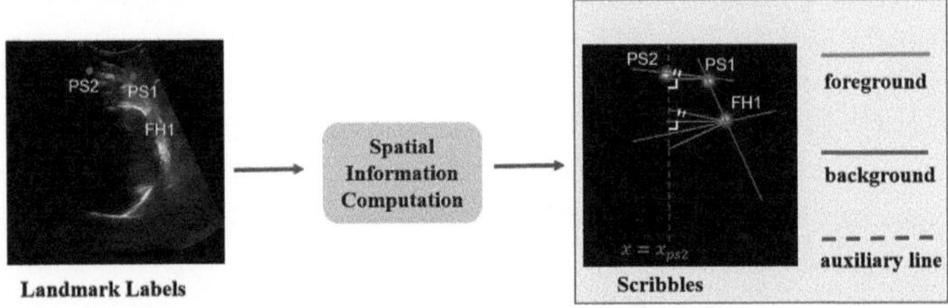

Fig. 3. The main process for measuring the Angle of Progression (AoP)

For the pubic symphysis (PS) region: since PS1 and PS2 are the two farthest points along the PS contour, the line connecting them must lie within the PS contour and thus can be used as a foreground scribble. Mathematically, let the pixel coordinates of PS1 and PS2 be denoted as PS1 $= (x_{ps1}, y_{ps1})$ and PS2 $= (x_{ps2}, y_{ps2})$ respectively. The line segment $L_{PS1\text{-}PS2}$ (serving as the foreground scribble) can be expressed in two-point form as:

$$\frac{y - y_{ps1}}{y_{ps2} - y_{ps1}} = \frac{x - x_{ps1}}{x_{ps2} - x_{ps1}}, \tag{1}$$

In contrast, the extended parts at both ends of this line can be used as background scribbles. The rays extending $L_{PS1\text{-}PS2}$ beyond PS2 (denoted as $L_{PS1\text{-}PS2}^{+}$) and beyond PS1 (denoted as $L_{PS1\text{-}PS2}^{-}$) are given by:

$$L_{PS1\text{-}PS2}^{+} : \frac{y - y_{ps2}}{y_{ps2} - y_{ps1}} = \frac{x - x_{ps2}}{x_{ps2} - x_{ps1}}, \tag{2}$$

$$L_{PS1\text{-}PS2}^{-} : \frac{y - y_{ps1}}{y_{ps2} - y_{ps1}} = \frac{x - x_{ps1}}{x_{ps2} - x_{ps1}}, \tag{3}$$

Additionally, in most cases, the contour of a normal pubic symphysis appears convex rather than concave in radiographic images [15]. Therefore, we first draw an auxiliary line perpendicular to the x-axis through PS2, which is expressed as $x = x_{ps2}$. Then, drawing a line perpendicular to this auxiliary line (one above and one below the auxiliary line) as foreground scribbles will introduce little or no noise, which can enhance the foreground segmentation result of ScribblePrompt.

Fetal Head (FH) Area. For the fetal head (FH) area, the labeled data only includes the third point (FH1), which is located at the tangent position of the FH area. Let the pixel coordinate of FH1 be $FH1 = (x_{\mathrm{fh1}}, y_{\mathrm{fh1}})$. After connecting PS1 and FH1, the line segment $L_{\mathrm{PS1\text{-}FH1}}$ (and its extended parts) all lie within the background region, so this line can be designated as a background scribble. The equation of $L_{\mathrm{PS1\text{-}FH1}}$ in two-point form is:

$$\frac{y - y_{\mathrm{ps1}}}{y_{\mathrm{fh1}} - y_{\mathrm{ps1}}} = \frac{x - x_{\mathrm{ps1}}}{x_{\mathrm{fh1}} - x_{\mathrm{ps1}}}, \tag{4}$$

Moreover, the FH area occupies a relatively large proportion of ultrasound images. When a perpendicular line is drawn from FH1 to the aforementioned auxiliary line $x = x_{\mathrm{ps2}}$, the segment of this perpendicular line (within the FH area) will lie entirely within the FH area with minimal error. Additionally, the lines parallel to the line connecting PS2 and PS1 also lie within the FH area. To make the segmentation result more consistent with the ground truth, we further adopt lines with included angles of $10°$ and $30°$ (relative to the reference line) as scribbles for the foreground region of the FH area. Let the perpendicular line from FH1 to $x = x_{\mathrm{ps2}}$ have a foot of perpendicular $H = (x_{\mathrm{ps2}}, y_{\mathrm{fh1}})$. The lines forming $10°$ and $30°$ with the perpendicular line $FH1 - H$ (serving as foreground scribbles) have slopes $\tan(10°) \approx 0.1763$, $\tan(170°) \approx -0.1763$, $\tan(30°) \approx 0.577$, $\tan(150°) \approx -0.577$ respectively. Their equations are:

$$y - y_{\mathrm{fh1}} = \pm 0.1763(x - x_{\mathrm{fh1}}) \quad \text{(for } 10° \text{ included angle)} \tag{5}$$

$$y - y_{\mathrm{fh1}} = \pm 0.577 \cdot (x - x_{\mathrm{fh1}}) \quad \text{(for } 30° \text{ included angle)} \tag{6}$$

We take the segments of these lines within the FH area as the foreground scribbles.

Generation of Pseudo Labels. After generating scribble prompts from landmarks, we input these prompts into the parameter-frozen ScribblePrompt model to obtain segmentation results for the two target regions. Although the foundation model produces coarse segmentation outputs, direct utilization of these results would introduce substantial noise due to the dense classification nature of segmentation tasks. However, since our algorithm's core goal is to obtain point labels, only the anatomical positional relationships of each region in ultrasound images are required. Thus, we extract roughly constrained bounding boxes from the segmentation results to train the YOLOv11 backbone network, facilitating regional feature extraction.

Prior Information Learning. To extract prior object detection information, we optimize YOLOv11 during the model learning process by integrating multiple loss components. These components jointly address the core tasks of object classification, bounding box regression, and object confidence estimation. The total loss function for object detection training is a weighted combination of three key loss terms: classification loss, bounding box regression loss, and object confidence loss, as defined in Eq. 7.

$$\mathcal{L}_{\text{detect}} = \lambda_{\text{cls}} \cdot \mathcal{L}_{\text{cls}} + \lambda_{\text{reg}} \cdot \mathcal{L}_{\text{reg}} + \lambda_{\text{conf}} \cdot \mathcal{L}_{\text{conf}} \tag{7}$$

where λ_{cls}, λ_{reg}, and λ_{conf} are cross-validated hyperparameters used to balance the contributions of each loss component. $\mathcal{L}_{\text{cls}}$ is the classification loss, which employs Cross-Entropy (CE) loss to ensure accurate classification of different types of landmarks:

$$\mathcal{L}_{\text{cls}}(y, \hat{y}) = -\frac{1}{N} \sum_{i=1}^{N} \sum_{c=1}^{C} y_{i,c} \log(\hat{y}_{i,c}) \tag{8}$$

$\mathcal{L}_{\text{conf}}$ denotes the object existence confidence loss, which uses Binary Cross-Entropy (BCE) loss to distinguish between valid bounding boxes and background regions:

$$\mathcal{L}_{\text{conf}} = -\frac{1}{N_{\text{obj}} + N_{\text{noobj}}} \left(\sum_{i \in \text{obj}} C_i \log(\hat{C}_i) + \sum_{i \in \text{noobj}} (1 - C_i) \log(1 - \hat{C}_i) \right) \tag{9}$$

$\mathcal{L}_{\text{reg}}$ represents the bounding box regression loss, which utilizes Mean Squared Error (MSE) loss to optimize the spatial alignment between predicted and ground-truth bounding boxes:

$$\mathcal{L}_{\text{reg}} = \sum_{i=1}^{N_{\text{obj}}} \mathbb{1}_{\text{obj}} \left[(x_i - \hat{x}_i)^2 + (y_i - \hat{y}_i)^2 + (w_i - \hat{w}_i)^2 + (h_i - \hat{h}_i)^2 \right] \tag{10}$$

In the above formulas: N denotes the total number of bounding boxes; $C = 2$ represents the total number of box categories; $y_i = (x_i, y_i, w_i, h_i)$ and $\hat{y}_i = (\hat{x}_i, \hat{y}_i, \hat{w}_i, \hat{h}_i)$ are the ground-truth and predicted coordinates (center (x, y) and dimensions (w, h)) of the i-th bounding box, respectively; $y_{i,c}$ and $\hat{y}_{i,c}$ denote the one-hot pseudo labels and predicted probability that the i-th box belongs to the c-th category, respectively; N_{obj} and N_{noobj} are the counts of positive (object-containing) and negative (background) boxes; C_i and $\hat{C}_i$ represent the ground-truth (1 for positive, 0 for negative) and predicted confidence scores of the i-th box; $\mathbb{1}_{\text{obj}}$ is an indicator function (1 for positive boxes, 0 otherwise);

2.3   Precise Landmark Detection Refine

Labeled Images Learning. After generating ROI detection pseudo labels, the backbone network YOLOv11 can extract anatomical prior information from ultrasound images, which makes it possible that during the refinement process, implicit associations between key points and anatomical structures are added, accelerating the training of the network.

In the landmark detection phase, we use a multi-task joint loss function, incorporating an auxiliary ROI object detection loss into the specialized regression loss for keypoint detection, which enables the network to simultaneously learn both tasks effectively, and the ROI detection can help the network concentrate on the spatial and semantic relationship of landmarks. For the landmarks l and the predicted landmarks $\hat{l}$, the specific formula is as follows:

$$\mathcal{L}_{\text{label}} = \mathcal{L}_{\text{reg}}(l, \hat{l}) + \alpha \cdot \mathcal{L}_{\text{detect}}(y, \hat{y}) \tag{11}$$

where α are the weight coefficients used to balance the loss components, $\mathcal{L}_{\text{reg}}$ represents the regression loss of landmarks, which can be calculated using the Mean Squared Error (MSE) to measure the spatial deviation between the predicted and ground-truth key points:

$$\mathcal{L}_{\text{loc}}(l, \hat{l}) = \frac{1}{N} \sum_{i=1}^{N} \left\| l_i - \hat{l}_i \right\|^2 \tag{12}$$

where N represents the number of key points.

Unlabeled Image Learning. After training the network on labeled data, the trained model was used to generate landmark pseudo-labels for the unlabeled dataset. By setting a threshold for the output confidence score, we excluded images where the network failed to make valid predictions, leaving only high-confidence pseudo-labeled data for subsequent training.

To further enhance the model's learning efficiency on pseudo-labeled data, we introduce information entropy to quantify the confidence of the model's predictions and incorporate this confidence into the loss function as a dynamic weight. During training, the confidence is incorporated into the loss function as a weight coefficient:

$$\mathcal{L}_{\text{unlabel}} = \mathcal{L}_{\text{reg}}(l, \hat{l}) + \mathcal{C}(p, \hat{p}) \cdot \mathcal{L}_{\text{reg}}(p, \hat{p}) \tag{13}$$

For the prediction result p output by the pre-trained network and the network prediction $\hat{p}$ obtained after introducing noise, the confidence $\mathcal{C}(p, \hat{p})$ is defined as:

$$\mathcal{C}(p, \hat{p}) = \frac{1}{4} \left(\frac{p \cdot \hat{p}}{\|p\| \cdot \|\hat{p}\|} + 1 \right) \tag{14}$$

where $p \cdot \hat{p}$ denotes the dot product of the two prediction vectors, and $\|p\|$, $\|\hat{p}\|$ represent the L2 norms of p and $\hat{p}$, respectively. The confidence $\mathcal{C}(p, \hat{p})$ ranges from $[0, 0.5]$, with values closer to 0.5 indicating higher consistency between the predictions before and after noise injection, thus reflecting a higher confidence in the predictions of the model on unlabeled data. This weighted loss mechanism allows the model to adaptively allocate learning resources during training using unlabeled data, thereby improving the robustness of landmark detection.

3 Experiments

3.1 Experimental Materials

Dataset. The experiment utilizes a transperineal ultrasound dataset provided by the Intrapartum Ultrasound Grand Challenge 2025 (IUGC 2025) [8], which contains 31,421 images with 300 labeled images. During training, the labeled data was randomly split into training and testing sets at a 9:1 ratio. Due to the test phase was already closed, we use metrics from the validation phase online as ablation and comparison experiment results.

Evaluation Metrics. We conducted a quantitative comparison using two standard landmark localization and parameter estimation evaluation metrics: Mean Radial Error (MRE) and Absolute Parameter Difference (APD) [22]. The former assesses the spatial localization accuracy of predicted landmark points relative to ground truth, while the latter evaluates the deviation between the estimated Angle of Polarization (AoP) (derived from predicted landmarks) and the ground truth AoP. The definitions of each metric are as follows:

$$\mathrm{MRE} = \frac{1}{N} \sum_{i=1}^{N} \sqrt{(x_i^{pred} - x_i^{gt})^2 + (y_i^{pred} - y_i^{gt})^2} \tag{15}$$

where (x_i^{pred}, y_i^{pred}) and (x_i^{gt}, y_i^{gt}) are the predicted and ground truth coordinates of the i-th landmark, and N is the total number of landmarks.

$$\mathrm{APD} = |\mathrm{AoP}^{pred} - \mathrm{AoP}^{gt}| \tag{16}$$

where AoP^{pred} and AoP^{gt} are the predicted and ground truth Angle of Pose, respectively.

Parameter Setting and Implementation. In the first training stage, we set a learning rate of 0.001, a batch size of 8, and trained for 100 epochs with images resized to 640×640. In the second training stage, we set a learning rate of 0.001, a total batch size of 8, a labeled batch size of 4, a unlabeled batch size of 4, and trained for 100 epochs with images resized to 640×640. The network was optimized using the SGD optimizer. For comparative experiments, we adhered to the same parameters. All experiments were carried out using PyTorch on an Nvidia 3090 GPU equipped with 24 GB of memory.

3.2 Ablation Study

Ablation studies were conducted to verify the effectiveness of each component in the proposed framework. Table 1 summarizes the performance of models with different design configurations, where Model A (Baseline) uses only YOLOv11, trained exclusively on labeled images for landmark detection; Model B incorporates a pre-training stage for coarse anatomical region prior learning, followed

Table 1. Quantitative ablation results of models with different network learning strategies. The baseline used is YOLOv11 with only the labeled images for training.

Model	Strategy			Metrics	
	Baseline	+ Coarse Prior	+ Unlabeled Learning	MRE (pixel) ↓	APD (degree) ↓
A	✓			31.8969	13.5713
B	✓	✓		21.2317	9.4166
C	✓	✓	✓	17.7447	7.6243

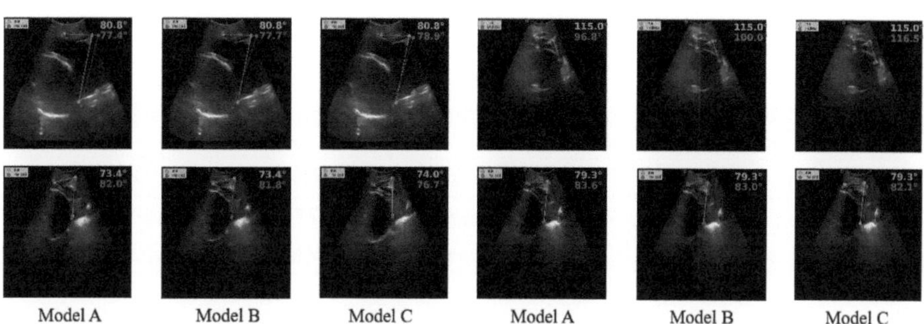

Model A   Model B   Model C   Model A   Model B   Model C

Fig. 4. Landmark detection results of different ablation models, green represents ground truth, red represents prediction results.

by fine-tuning the pre-trained YOLOv11 on labeled images for landmark detection; Model C builds on Model B by adding a confidence-weighted loss term for unlabeled images during the training process.

Effectiveness of Coarse Prior Anatomical Area Learning. As shown in Table 1, by comparing Model A and Model B, it can be observed that the integration of the Coarse Prior Anatomical Area Learning module enables the network to capture the correlations between different regions in ultrasound images, leading to a significant improvement in the detection accuracy of key landmarks. Specifically, the MRE decreases substantially from 31.8969 to 21.2317, and the APD also reduces from 13.5713 to 9.4166.

The visualization results in Fig. 4 further confirm that after incorporating anatomical prior learning, each landmark predicted by the network is closer to the ground truth. In particular, the detection performance for the FH1 landmark has been remarkably enhanced.

Effectiveness of Precise Landmark Detection Refine. As shown in Table 1, by comparing Model B and Model C, it can be seen that after incorporating unlabeled images into the network training via the confidence-weighted loss during the refinement stage, the network's key landmark detection performance is further improved. Specifically, the MRE decreases from 21.2317 to 17.7447, and the APD reduces from 9.4166 to 7.6243. These results verify the effectiveness of the semi-supervised strategy proposed in this study.

The visualization results in Fig. 4 demonstrate that after introducing the confidence-weighted loss, the AoP predicted by the network is more consistent with the ground truth.

3.3   Comparison Study

We evaluated the AoP measurement performance of our proposed framework and compared it with several fully-supervised methods and semi-supervised methods: 1) Unet [18]; 2) Cenet [20]; 3) YOLOv11 [11]; 4) Mean Teacher [21] ; 5) Adversarial Network [27]; 6)DFGC [25].

Table 2. Quantitative results of different comparison networks.

Supervision	Model	Task type	MRE (pixel) ↓	APD (degree) ↓
Fully-supervised	UNet	Regression	26.7731	10.4903
	UNet	Classification	24.2149	10.1297
	CENet	Regression	27.6230	9.8838
	CENet	Classification	20.7143	8.4383
	YOLOv11	Regression	31.8969	13.5713
Semi-supervised	Mean teacher	Classification	27.7819	10.3221
	Adversarial network	Classification	32.6527	14.2298
	DFGC	Classification	24.7469	9.1388
	ours	Regression	**17.7447**	**7.6243**

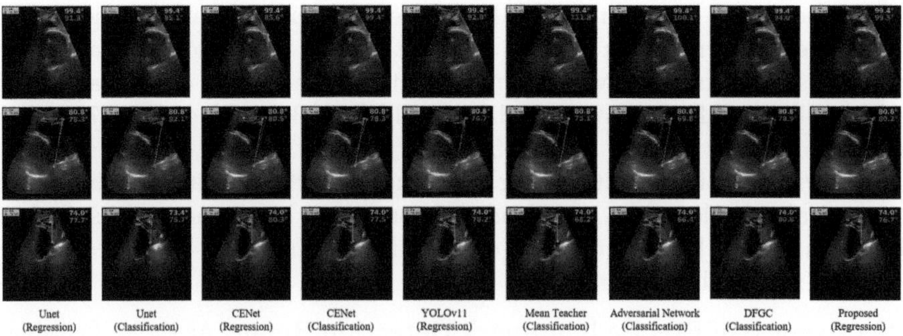

Fig. 5. Landmark detection results of different comparison methods, green represents ground truth, red represents prediction results.

As presented in Table 2, different algorithms exhibit varying landmark detection performances when adopting distinct learning strategies. For the Unet and

CENet algorithms, compared with direct coordinate regression tasks (which directly obtain landmark coordinates), using heatmaps for image classification tasks achieves a reduction in MRE by 2.5582 and 6.9087, respectively, with the APD also decreasing by more than 0.3. The nnUNet algorithm, which employs heatmaps for classification, yields better metrics than CENet. When used independently, YOLOv11 shows slightly inferior performance compared to other fully supervised algorithms. For the Mean Teacher algorithm and Adversarial Network applied to landmark detection with UNet as its backbone, the extremely limited information in heatmaps generated from key points prevents the algorithm from learning effective features, resulting in excessively large MRE and APD values that render it unable to detect target points effectively. The DFGC algorithm, specifically designed for ultrasound images, can learn target-related features effectively (achieving an MRE of 24.7469 and an APD of 9.1388) but still performs less favorably than the algorithm proposed in this study.

Figure 5 further confirms that the proposed algorithm achieves significant improvements in detecting the PS1 and PS2 landmarks compared to other algorithms. For FH1 detection, the algorithm substantially enhances positional accuracy, ensuring that FH1 is located as close as possible on the fetal head contour–avoiding mislocalization within the FH region–and thus enabling more accurate calculation of the AoP.

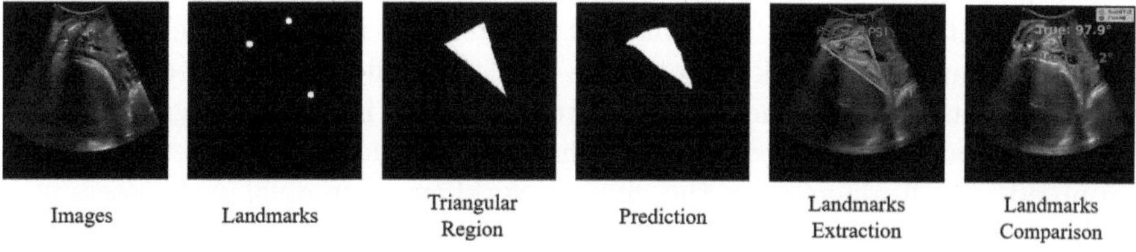

Fig. 6. Schematic diagram of learning landmark detection from the triangular region composed of landmarks.

4   Discussion

During the competition, our experiments revealed notable findings: combining a semi-supervised framework with the standard UNet drastically degrades landmark detection performance, as evidenced by substantial worsening of metrics like MRE and angular offset mean absolute error (APD) (exceeding 100). This underscores the limitations of generic encoder-decoder architectures for semi-supervised intrapartum ultrasound measurements. The core issue likely stems from the sparsity and ambiguity of ultrasound keypoints–semi-supervised pseudo-labels generated from unlabeled data tend to propagate noise when learning from isolated, context-poor points. While UNet excels at dense pixel-wise segmentation, it fails to capture sparse, high-resolution spatial cues critical for keypoint localization, instead overfitting irrelevant background textures or blurred boundaries and amplifying distance/angle estimation errors.

In contrast, integrating a regional background (e.g., the PS1-PS2-FH1 triangle) defined by three key landmarks with a conventional encoder-decoder architecture significantly improves detection accuracy. This method incorporates spatial priors, framing the task as regional feature extraction rather than isolated point regression. This approach provides richer contextual information, such as relative positional relationships and boundary transitions between the pubic symphysis and fetal head. The proposed encoder-decoder architecture is optimized for hierarchical feature aggregation, enabling more effective regional pattern learning, reducing keypoint ambiguity, and enhancing the robustness of distance and angle estimation.

Based on the advantages of introducing regional background information, future work can further optimize models based on regional feature extraction. Explore how to combine multi-level spatial prior knowledge, utilize geometric relationships and semantic information between key points, not limited to the connection of three landmark points, but also consider more complex regional constraints, thereby further improving detection accuracy and model robustness.

5   Conclusion

This study focuses on addressing the limitations of manual Angle of Progression measurement in intrapartum ultrasound and tackles the core challenges faced by automated AoP landmark measurement methods: the reliance on massive manual landmark annotations and the difficulty of detecting minute fetal head anatomical landmarks. To resolve these issues, a progressive semi-supervised landmark detection algorithm for automated AoP measurement is proposed, which aligns with the clinical workflow of manual AoP assessment. In the first stage, spatial information of key landmarks is leveraged to generate foreground/background scribbles for the pubic symphysis and fetal head. These scribbles are input to the frozen ScribblePrompt segmentation foundation model to obtain coarse segmentation results, which serve as pseudo-labels to guide the network in focusing on key anatomical regions. In the second stage, the network extracts anatomical priors from ultrasound images. It undergoes fine-tuning via weight-allocated learning on both labeled and unlabeled data–effectively reducing the demand for annotated data while enhancing the model's ability to learn discriminative features of minute landmarks. Experimental results confirm that the proposed algorithm achieves favorable performance in key anatomical landmark detection, laying a solid foundation for accurate automated AoP measurement. By integrating anatomical prior learning and semi-supervised learning, the algorithm not only mitigates the dependency on manual annotation but also improves the robustness of landmark detection against tissue confusion, thereby providing a clinically valuable tool for objective, standardized, and efficient AoP assessment during labor.

References

1. Bai, J., Lekadir, K., Ni, D., Slimani, S., Campello, V.M., Ohene-Botwe, B., Lu, Y., Chen, G., Hou, H., Qiu, D., Zhou, Z.: Intrapartum ultrasound grand challenge 2024. In: 27th International Conference on Medical Image Computing and Computer Assisted Intervention (MICCAI 2024), Zenodo (2024). https://doi.org/10.5281/zenodo.10979813

2. Bai, J., Ou, Z., Lu, Y., Ni, D., Chen, G.: Pubic symphysis-fetal head segmentation from transperineal ultrasound images. In: International Conference on Medical Image Computing and Computer Assisted Intervention (MICCAI) (2023)

3. Bai, J., Sun, Z., Yu, S., Lu, Y., Long, S., Wang, H., Qiu, R., Ou, Z., Zhou, M., Zhi, D., et al.: A framework for computing angle of progression from transperineal ultrasound images for evaluating fetal head descent using a novel double branch network. Front. Physiol. **13**, 940150 (2022)

4. Bai, J., Zhou, Z., Ou, Z., Koehler, G., Stock, R., Maier-Hein, K., Elbatel, M., Martí, R., Li, X., Qiu, Y., et al.: PSFHS challenge report: pubic symphysis and fetal head segmentation from intrapartum ultrasound images. Med. Image Anal. **99**, 103353 (2025)

5. Chen, G., Bai, J., Ou, Z., Lu, Y., Wang, H.: PSFHS: intrapartum ultrasound image dataset for AI-based segmentation of pubic symphysis and fetal head. Sci. Data **11**(1), 436 (2024)

6. Chen, Z., Lu, Y., Long, S., Campello, V.M., Bai, J., Lekadir, K.: Fetal head and pubic symphysis segmentation in intrapartum ultrasound image using a dual-path boundary-guided residual network. IEEE J. Biomed. Health Inform. **28**(8), 4648–4659 (2024)

7. Chen, Z., Ou, Z., Lu, Y., Bai, J.: Direction-guided and multi-scale feature screening for fetal head-pubic symphysis segmentation and angle of progression calculation. Expert Syst. Appl. **245**, 123096 (2024)

8. CodaBench: Iugc2025: International unsupervised geospatial challenge (2025). https://www.codabench.org/competitions/7105/. Accessed 30 Aug. 2025

9. Haws, R.A., Yakoob, M.Y., Soomro, T., Menezes, E.V., Darmstadt, G.L., Bhutta, Z.A.: Reducing stillbirths: screening and monitoring during pregnancy and labour. BMC Pregnancy Childbirth **9**(Suppl 1), S5 (2009)

10. Jiang, J., Wang, H., Bai, J., Long, S., Chen, S., Campello, V.M., Lekadir, K.: Intrapartum ultrasound image segmentation of pubic symphysis and fetal head using dual student-teacher framework with CNN-VIT collaborative learning. In: International Conference on Medical Image Computing and Computer-Assisted Intervention, pp. 448–458. Springer (2024)

11. Khanam, R., Hussain, M.: YOLOv11: an overview of the key architectural enhancements (2024). arXiv preprint arXiv:2410.17725

12. Lu, Y., Zhi, D., Zhou, M., Lai, F., Chen, G., Ou, Z., Zeng, R., Long, S., Qiu, R., Zhou, M., et al.: Multitask deep neural network for the fully automatic measurement of the angle of progression. Comput. Math. Methods Med. **2022**(1), 5192338 (2022)

13. Lu, Y., Zhou, M., Zhi, D., Zhou, M., Jiang, X., Qiu, R., Ou, Z., Wang, H., Qiu, D., Zhong, M., et al.: The JNU-IFM dataset for segmenting pubic symphysis-fetal head. Data Brief **41**, 107904 (2022)

14. Ou, Z., Bai, J., Chen, Z., Lu, Y., Wang, H., Long, S., Chen, G.: Rtseg-net: a lightweight network for real-time segmentation of fetal head and pubic symphysis from intrapartum ultrasound images. Comput. Biol. Med. **175**, 108501 (2024)

15. van Ovost, A., Hanff, D.F., Serner, A., van Klij, P., Agricola, R., Weir, A.: Radiographic assessment of the pubic symphysis in elite male adolescent football players: development and reliability of the maturing adolescent pubic symphysis (maps) classification. Eur. J. Radiol. **167**, 111068 (2023)

16. Payer, C., Štern, D., Bischof, H., Urschler, M.: Regressing heatmaps for multiple landmark localization using CNNs. In: International Conference on Medical Image Computing and Computer-Assisted Intervention, pp. 230–238. Springer (2016)

17. Qiu, R., Zhou, M., Bai, J., Lu, Y., Wang, H.: PSFHSP-Net: an efficient lightweight network for identifying pubic symphysis-fetal head standard plane from intrapartum ultrasound images. Med. Biol. Eng. Comput. **62**(10), 2975–2986 (2024)

18. Ronneberger, O., Fischer, P., Brox, T.: U-Net: convolutional networks for biomedical image segmentation. In: Medical Image Computing and Computer-Assisted Intervention–MICCAI 2015: 18th International Conference, Munich, Germany, October 5–9, 2015, Proceedings, Part III, vol. 18, pp. 234–241. Springer (2015)

19. Sofka, M., Milletari, F., Jia, J., Rothberg, A.: Fully convolutional regression network for accurate detection of measurement points. In: International Workshop on Deep Learning in Medical Image Analysis, pp. 258–266. Springer (2017)

20. Tao, H., Xie, C., Wang, J., Xin, Z.: CENet: a channel-enhanced spatiotemporal network with sufficient supervision information for recognizing industrial smoke emissions. IEEE Internet Things J. **9**(19), 18749–18759 (2022)

21. Tarvainen, A., Valpola, H.: Mean teachers are better role models: weight-averaged consistency targets improve semi-supervised deep learning results. In: Advances in Neural Information Processing Systems, vol. 30 (2017)

22. Wang, C.W., Huang, C.T., Hsieh, M.C., Li, C.H., Chang, S.W., Li, W.C., Vandaele, R., Marée, R., Jodogne, S., Geurts, P., et al.: Evaluation and comparison of anatomical landmark detection methods for cephalometric X-ray images: a grand challenge. IEEE Trans. Med. Imaging **34**(9), 1890–1900 (2015)

23. Wang, X., Xiao, F., Li, J.: Intrapartum ultrasound monitoring in second-stage labor: impact on delivery outcomes. J. Radiat. Res. Appl. Sci. **18**(4), 101846 (2025)

24. Wong, H.E., Rakic, M., Guttag, J., Dalca, A.V.: Scribbleprompt: fast and flexible interactive segmentation for any biomedical image. In: European Conference on Computer Vision, pp. 207–229. Springer (2024)

25. Yao, Y., Duan, X., Qu, A., Chen, M., Chen, J., Chen, L.: DFCG: a dual-frequency cascade graph model for semi-supervised ultrasound image segmentation with diffusion model. Knowl.-Based Syst. **300**, 112261 (2024)

26. Yin, S., Wang, S., Chen, X., Chen, E., Liang, C.: Attentive one-dimensional heatmap regression for facial landmark detection and tracking. In: Proceedings of the 28th ACM International Conference on Multimedia, pp. 538–546 (2020)

27. Zhang, Y., Yang, L., Chen, J., Fredericksen, M., Hughes, D.P., Chen, D.Z.: Deep adversarial networks for biomedical image segmentation utilizing unannotated images. In: International Conference on Medical Image Computing and Computer-Assisted Intervention, pp. 408–416. Springer (2017)

28. Zhou, M., Yuan, C., Chen, Z., Wang, C., Lu, Y.: Automatic angle of progress measurement of intrapartum transperineal ultrasound image with deep learning. In: International Conference on Medical Image Computing and Computer-Assisted Intervention, pp. 406–414. Springer (2020)

29. Zhou, Z., Lu, Y.: Baseline method at the intrapartum ultrasound grand challenge 2024. In: Intrapartum Ultrasound Grand Challenge, pp. 1–10. Springer (2024)

30. Zhou, Z., Lu, Y., Bai, J., Campello, V.M., Feng, F., Lekadir, K.: Segment anything model for fetal head-pubic symphysis segmentation in intrapartum ultrasound image analysis. Expert Syst. Appl. **263**, 125699 (2025)

Pseudo-label Enhanced TransUNet for Robust Landmark Localization in Intrapartum Ultrasound

Xuezhi Zhang[1,2,3,4], Xi Chen[1,2,3,4], Hao Yan[5], Lyuyang Tong[1,2,3,4(✉)], and Bo Du[1,2,3,4(✉)]

[1] School of Computer Science, Wuhan University, Wuhan, China
`{Lyuyangtong,dubo}@whu.edu.cn`
[2] National Engineering Research Center for Multimedia Software, Wuhan University, Wuhan, China
[3] Institute of Artificial Intelligence, School of Computer Science, Wuhan University, Wuhan, China
[4] Hubei Key Laboratory of Multimedia and Network Communication Engineering, Wuhan University, Wuhan, China
[5] Key Laboratory of Aerospace Information Security and Trusted Computing, Ministry of Education, School of Cyber Science and Engineering, Wuhan University, Wuhan, China

Abstract. Accurate and reliable detection of anatomical landmarks in intrapartum ultrasound is a critical component of quantitative and objective assessment of fetal head descent, which plays an essential role in guiding clinical decision-making during labor. However, manual annotation of ultrasound images is time-consuming, requires expert knowledge, and suffers from inter-observer variability. Moreover, the scarcity of fully annotated datasets poses additional challenges for training high-performance deep learning models in this domain. To address these challenges, we propose a three-stage framework that effectively leverages both fully labeled and partially labeled data to improve landmark detection performance. In Stage 1, a TransUNet model is pre-trained on a large-scale video-derived segmentation dataset and iteratively fine-tuned on point-annotated images using an error-weighted loss strategy. Stage 2 incorporates high-confidence pseudo-labeled data generated by the refined model, with post-processing applied to ensure label quality. Stage 3 fuses predictions from three independently trained TransUNet models via averaging to enhance stability and robustness. Experimental results on the IUGC 2025 Landmark Detection Challenge test set demonstrate that our method achieves an Average Point Distance of 13.28 pixels and an AOP MAE of 3.87 degrees, demonstrating the effectiveness of semi-supervised learning and model ensembling for intrapartum ultrasound landmark detection.

Keywords: Intrapartum Ultrasound · Landmark Detection · Semi-supervised Learning · Pseudo-labeling

J. Bai et al. (Eds.): IUGC 2025, LNCS 16317, pp. 77–87, 2026.
https://doi.org/10.1007/978-3-032-11616-1_7

1   Introduction

Intrapartum ultrasound is an important imaging tool for real-time assessment of labor progression, offering more objective and reproducible information than traditional clinical examinations. Key anatomical landmarks—such as the fetal head and pubic symphysis—are essential for deriving clinically relevant measurements like the angle of progression (AoP) and headperineum distance, which guide decisions on labor management.

Manual annotation of these landmarks requires expert knowledge, is time-consuming, and suffers from inter- and intra-observer variability, limiting large-scale clinical adoption. Fully automated landmark localization has thus become a pressing research goal. Traditional image processing methods (e.g., active shape models, Hough transforms) struggle with the noisy, low-contrast, and variable appearance of intrapartum ultrasound.

Deep learning methods, particularly convolutional neural networks (CNNs) and Transformer-based models, have shown strong performance in medical image analysis. U-Net [16] is a widely adopted encoderdecoder architecture with skip connections that effectively fuses multi-scale features for precise pixel-level predictions. TransUNet [8] extends U-Net by incorporating Vision Transformers into the encoder, combining CNN-based local feature extraction with global context modeling—an advantage in ultrasound landmark detection, where relevant structures may be distant or partially occluded.

Despite these advances, several challenges remain in applying deep learning models to intrapartum ultrasound. Ultrasound images are inherently noisy and exhibit poor contrast, making it difficult to distinguish anatomical boundaries. Furthermore, the scarcity of large annotated datasets limits the effectiveness of supervised learning frameworks. Therefore, there is a growing demand for data-efficient and architecture-robust solutions that can achieve high localization accuracy while accommodating the unique characteristics of intrapartum ultrasound.

In this study, we propose a fully automated three-stage framework for fetal landmark localization and AoP estimation from intrapartum ultrasound images. Our method leverages a progressive pseudo-labeling strategy to exploit unlabeled data and improve robustness. Specifically, we first pretrain a TransUNet-based segmentation model using manually labeled video keyframes and then refine it with pseudo labels from point-supervised images (Stage 1). Next, we perform progressive pseudo labeling with confidence-based filtering to incrementally incorporate high-quality unlabeled samples into training (Stage 2). Finally, we apply a weighted ensemble strategy, where each model independently predicts the segmentation mask and three anatomical landmarks, and their outputs are averaged to compute the AoP (Stage 3). Our contributions are summarized as follows:

- We propose a fully automatic framework for fetal head progression assessment in intrapartum ultrasound, which jointly performs anatomical landmark localization and AoP estimation.

- We design a three-stage pseudo-labeling strategy to leverage both labeled and unlabeled data, enhancing the effectiveness of training.
- We integrate a simple yet robust geometry-based module for AoP measurement based on three key landmarks, ensuring interpretability and clinical relevance.

In this work, we aim to support the technical implementation of the WHO Labour Care Guide and promote safer, more standardized labor monitoring practices via automated ultrasound analysis.

2   Method

As illustrated in Fig. 1, our approach consists of three main components: 1) pretraining and label refinement; 2) progressive pseudo labeling with confidence filtering; and 3) model ensembling and final AoP estimation.

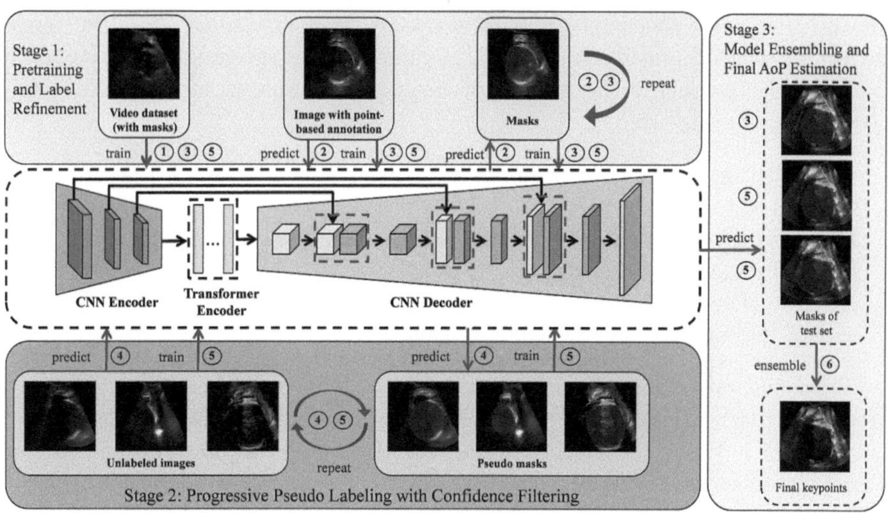

Fig. 1. Overview of the proposed framework.

2.1   Stage 1: Pretraining and Label Refinement

The first stage of our framework, illustrated in Fig. 2, consists of a pretraining phase followed by iterative label refinement. We leverage the video dataset provided by the MICCAI IUGC 2024: Intrapartum Ultrasound Grand Challenge [2,4,10,12,13]. Specifically, we extract 2,562 key frames with corresponding segmentation masks from the videos as a pretraining dataset. A TransUNet

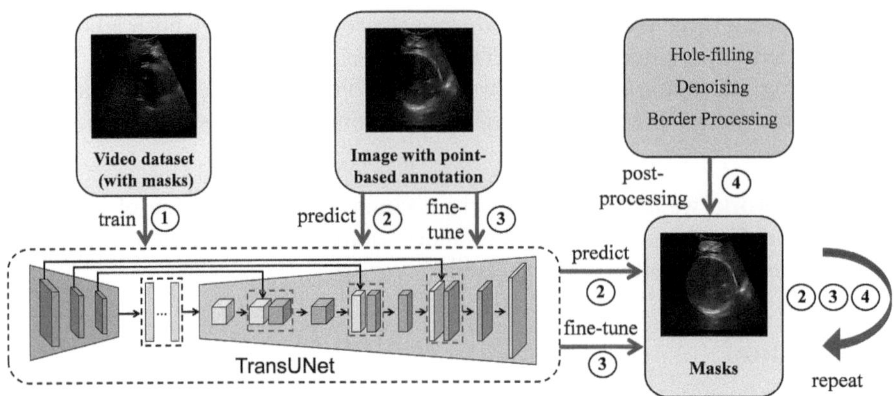

Fig. 2. Illustration of stage 1: pe-training and label refinement.

model [8] is pre-trained on this dataset to learn robust anatomical representations. The pre-trained model is then used to generate masks for 300 images with point-based annotations (i.e., three annotated keypoints but no segmentation masks). To ensure the quality of these predictions, we apply a three-step post-processing pipeline:

- **Hole-filling:** Connected component analysis is used to fill holes within the segmented regions.
- **Denoising:** Only the largest connected component is retained, and small isolated regions are removed.
- **Border Processing:** Boundary-connected components are corrected to ensure the integrity of the segmentation mask.

Following post-processing, we compute the anatomical keypoints from each predicted mask (detailed in Stage 3), and measure the Euclidean distance between each predicted keypoint and its corresponding annotated location. These distances are then used to assign sample-specific loss weights during fine-tuning, where samples with larger prediction errors contribute less to the overall loss. Specifically, for the i-th sample, the loss weight w_i is defined as:

$$w_i = \exp\left(-\lambda \cdot \frac{1}{3} \sum_{j=1}^{3} \left| \mathbf{p}_{i,j} - \hat{\mathbf{p}}_{i,j} \right|_2 \right) \tag{1}$$

where $\mathbf{p}_{i,j}$ and $\hat{\mathbf{p}}_{i,j}$ denote the predicted and annotated coordinates of the j-th keypoint for the i-th sample, and λ is a scaling factor controlling the sensitivity to prediction error. This re-weighted fine-tuning process is iterated for three rounds, gradually refining the model using both the initial pseudo-labels and the spatial alignment between predicted and annotated landmarks. The final output of Stage 1 is a refined TransUNet model with improved segmentation quality tailored to point-supervised images.

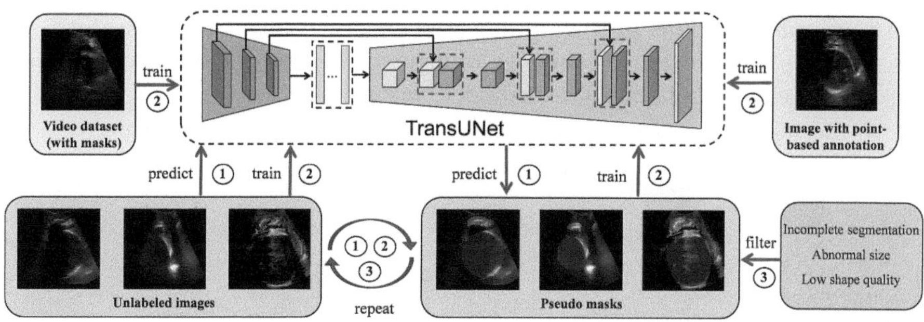

Fig. 3. Illustration of stage 2: progressive pseudo labeling with confidence filtering.

2.2   Stage 2: Progressive Pseudo Labeling with Confidence Filtering

In the second stage, we implement a progressive pseudo labeling strategy to exploit the unlabeled dataset more effectively. As illustrated in Fig. 3, all unlabeled images are evenly split into three subsets. The fine-tuned model from Stage 1 is then used to generate segmentation masks for the first subset.

To ensure the quality of the pseudo labels, we apply a filtering process to remove unreliable masks based on the following criteria:

- **Incomplete segmentation:** Masks that contain only one or zero connected regions are discarded.
- **Abnormal size:** Masks whose area significantly deviates from the mean area of all labeled masks are discarded. Specifically, we discard masks whose area is either larger than 1.5× the mean or smaller than 0.5× the mean.
- **Low shape quality:** Masks with a fetal head mask shape factor less than 0.8 are removed. The shape factor is defined as:

$$\text{Shape Factor} = \frac{4\pi \times \text{Area}}{(\text{Perimeter})^2} \tag{2}$$

After filtering, the remaining high-quality pseudo-labeled samples from the first subset are combined with two fully labeled datasets: the manually labeled video keyframes and the corrected masks from Stage 1. To balance the contribution of different data sources, we apply different loss weights during training. Specifically, the total loss is computed as:

$$\mathcal{L}_{\text{total}} = \mathcal{L}_{\text{video}} + \mathcal{L}_{\text{stage1}} + 0.5 \times \mathcal{L}_{\text{pseudo}} \tag{3}$$

where $\mathcal{L}_{\text{video}}$ refers to the loss from the manually labeled video keyframes, $\mathcal{L}_{\text{stage1}}$ denotes the loss from the corrected pseudo labels generated in Stage 1, and $\mathcal{L}_{\text{pseudo}}$ represents the loss from the newly generated pseudo-labeled data in this stage.

The model trained on this combined dataset is then used to generate masks for the second subset of unlabeled data, followed by the same filtering and retraining process. This process is repeated once more to handle the third subset, forming a three-step progressive refinement framework that incrementally improves pseudo-label quality and model performance.

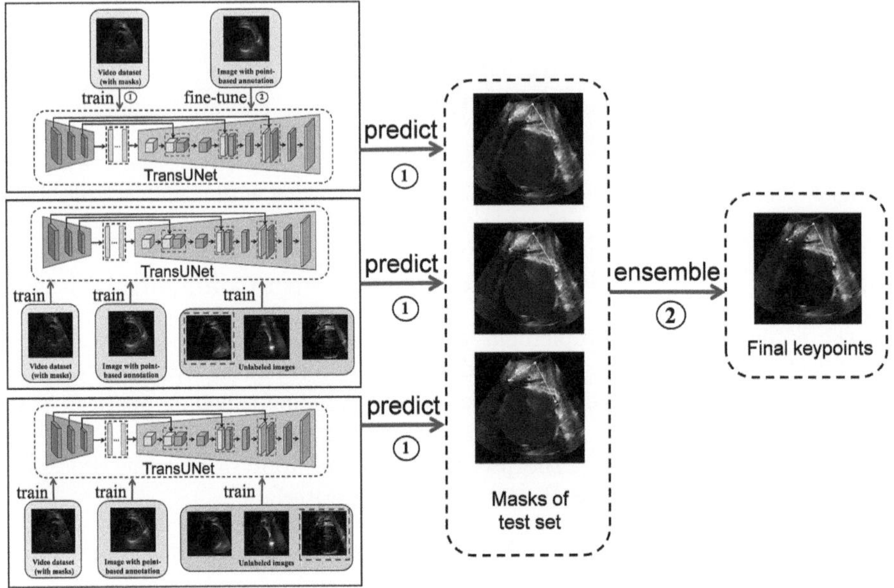

Fig. 4. Illustration of stage 3: model ensembling and final AoP estimation.

2.3   Stage 3: Model Ensembling and Final AoP Estimation

In the final stage, we adopt a model ensembling strategy to enhance segmentation robustness and measurement consistency. As shown in Fig. 4, we employ an ensemble of three models: (1) the fine-tuned model from Stage 1, and (2)(3) two models trained respectively on the first and third subsets in Stage 2. Each model independently generates segmentation masks for the test set.

The predicted masks are first refined using the same post-processing pipeline introduced in Stage 1, which includes hole filling, denoising, and boundary correction. Based on the refined binary masks, we extract three anatomical keypoints required for computing the Angle of Progression (AoP): two points on the pubic symphysis contour (PS1 and PS2), and one tangential point on the fetal head contour (FH1). The extraction procedures are described below as pseudocode (Algorithm 1).

Each model predicts a set of coordinates for the three keypoints: PS1, PS2, and FH1. To reduce prediction variance, we adopt a coordinate-wise averaging strategy across the three models:

$$\text{Keypoint}_{final} = \frac{1}{3} \sum_{m=1}^{3} \text{Keypoint}_m \tag{4}$$

where Keypoint_m represents the coordinates predicted by the m-th model. This straightforward fusion improves robustness and ensures stable keypoint localization results.

Algorithm 1. Extraction of PS1, PS2, and FH1

Require: Binary mask M_{ps} of pubic symphysis (label 1), binary mask M_{fh} of fetal head (label 2)
Ensure: Coordinates $(PS1_x, PS1_y)$, $(PS2_x, PS2_y)$, $(FH1_x, FH1_y)$
 1: $C_{ps} \leftarrow$ FindLargestContour(M_{ps})
 2: $P_{ps} \leftarrow$ ExtractContourPoints(C_{ps})
 3: $(p_a, p_b) \leftarrow$ FindFurthestPointPair(P_{ps})
 4: **if** $p_a.x > p_b.x$ **then**
 5:     $PS1 \leftarrow p_a$, $PS2 \leftarrow p_b$
 6: **else**
 7:     $PS1 \leftarrow p_b$, $PS2 \leftarrow p_a$
 8: **end if**
 9: $C_{fh} \leftarrow$ ExtractContourPoints(M_{fh})
10: $FH1 \leftarrow \arg\min_{p \in C_{fh}} \text{Angle}(\overrightarrow{PS1p}, \text{NormalVector}(p))$
11: **if** $FH1$ is not valid **then**
12:     $FH1 \leftarrow$ FindRightmostPoint(C_{fh})
13: **end if**
14: **return** $PS1, PS2, FH1$

---

3   Experiments

3.1   Dataset Description

Our experiments are conducted on the benchmark dataset provided by the **Landmark Detection Challenge for Intrapartum Ultrasound Measurement (IUGC 2025)** [1–7,9–15,17] , which focuses on automatic landmark detection in fetal ultrasound images to assist clinical assessment of labor progression. The dataset is divided into the following subsets:

- **Training Set:** 31,421 ultrasound images in total, among which 300 images are manually annotated with three anatomical landmarks for supervised learning. The remaining unlabeled images are used for semi-supervised learning.
- **Validation Set:** 100 annotated images used to validate model performance during training.
- **Test Set:** 501 hidden images used for final evaluation by the challenge organizers.

In addition, we utilize an external dataset from the **MICCAI IUGC 2024: Intrapartum Ultrasound Grand Challenge** to improve the robustness of our segmentation model through pretraining. This dataset consists of:

- **Standard Plane Videos:** 288 videos composed entirely of standard planes, from which 24,434 frames are extracted, including 2,906 frames with segmentation masks.
- **Non-standard Plane Videos:** 168 videos consisting of non-standard planes, contributing 31,450 additional frames without segmentation labels.

This external video dataset serves as the foundation for initial model pretraining and label refinement in Stage 1 of our framework.

3.2 Experimental Setup

All experiments are conducted on two NVIDIA GeForce RTX 4090 GPUs. The network is trained in three stages: (1) 200 epochs of pretraining, (2) 100 epochs of fine-tuning on labeled data, and (3) 300 epochs of pseudo-label-based training.

We adopt stochastic gradient descent (SGD) with an initial learning rate of 0.07, which is decayed during training. The batch size is set to 16 throughout all stages. The input images are resized to 512×512, and the following data augmentation strategies are employed:

- **Random Horizontal Flip:** Applied with 50% probability.
- **Random Rotation:** Random rotation within $\pm 10°$ using bilinear interpolation.
- **Color Jittering:** Brightness and contrast adjusted within a variation range of 0.1.

The base segmentation loss is a weighted combination of cross-entropy loss and Dice loss, defined as:

$$\mathcal{L}_{seg} = 0.5 \cdot \mathcal{L}_{CE} + 0.5 \cdot \mathcal{L}_{Dice} \tag{5}$$

To account for different data sources, we apply stage-specific loss scaling factors λ to balance contributions from labeled and pseudo-labeled samples. The detailed formulation can be found in the Method section.

Table 1. Quantitative evaluation results on the validation set.

Models	MSE	MAE	Average Point Distance	PS1 Distance	PS2 Distance	Tangency Distance	AOP MSE	AOP MAE
Pre-trained Model	417.60	10.96	17.37	10.89	14.60	26.60	213.26	8.16
Fine-tuned Model	260.55	8.68	13.80	9.10	8.99	23.32	152.36	5.98
Model with Pseudo-labels	247.50	8.23	13.04	8.04	8.63	22.45	124.75	5.31
Ensemble Model	225.51	7.99	12.67	7.77	8.56	21.67	128.00	5.30

3.3   Experimental Results

Table 1 presents the quantitative evaluation results for all models across different evaluation metrics. We report the overall Mean Squared Error (MSE), Mean Absolute Error (MAE), average distance error of three keypoints (PS1, PS2, and Tangency), as well as the MSE and MAE of the AoP angle.

As shown in Table 1, the fine-tuned model significantly outperforms the pretrained model, with the average keypoint distance reduced from 17.37 px to 13.80 px. Incorporating pseudo-labeled data further boosts performance, especially in the AoP angle estimation, where the MSE decreases from 152.36 to 124.75. The ensemble model achieves the best overall performance, reducing the average keypoint error to 12.67 px and the AoP MAE to 5.30, demonstrating that model fusion effectively mitigates prediction variance and enhances robustness.

Figure 5 visualizes representative segmentation results and predicted keypoints for different models. As shown, the pseudo-label model produces more accurate and stable keypoint locations, closely aligning with the ground truth and yielding smoother AoP angle estimation.

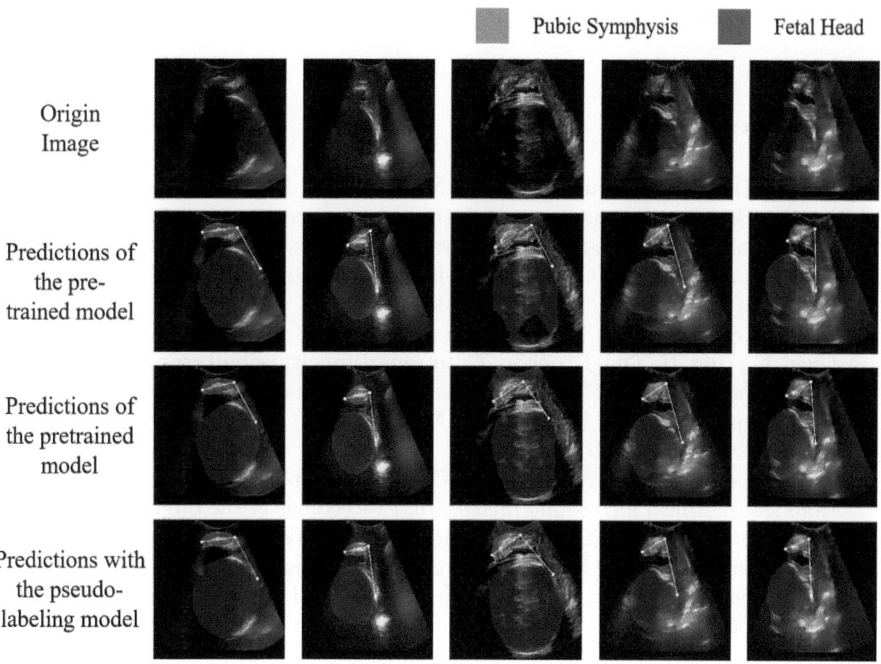

Fig. 5. Visualization results of segmentation and keypoints.

4   Conclusion

In this work, we proposed a three-stage framework for accurate landmark detection in intrapartum ultrasound images. Starting from a pre-trained TransUNet model, we refined labels through an iterative error-weighted fine-tuning strategy and further leveraged pseudo-labeled data to enhance generalization. Experimental results on the IUGC 2025 dataset demonstrate consistent performance gains at each stage. The proposed approach effectively bridges the gap between limited high-quality annotations and abundant unlabeled data, offering a practical and scalable solution for clinical labor progress assessment.

Acknowledgements. This work was supported in part by the National Key Research and Development Program of China under Grants 2023YFC2705700, the National Natural Science Foundation of China under Grants 62306217 and 62225113, the Postdoctoral Fellowship Program of CPSF under Grant Number GZC20231987, the China Postdoctoral Science Foundation under Grant Number 2024T170686 and 2024M752471, the Major Program (JD) of Hubei Province (2023BAA017), the Innovative Research Group Project of Hubei Province under Grants 2024AFA017. The numerical calculations in this paper have been done on the supercomputing system in the Supercomputing Center of Wuhan University.

References

1. Bai, J., Khobo, I., Slimani, S., Lu, Y., Ni, D., Yaqub, M., Lekadir, K., Ma, J., Li, S.: Landmark detection challenge for intrapartum ultrasound measurement meeting the actual clinical assessment of labor progress. In: Proceedings of the Medical Image Computing and Computer Assisted Intervention (MICCAI 2025). Springer (2025). https://doi.org/10.5281/zenodo.15172238
2. Bai, J., Lekadir, K., Ni, D., Slimani, S., Campello, V.M., Ohene-Botwe, B., Lu, Y., Chen, G., Hou, H., Qiu, D., Zhou, Z.: Intrapartum ultrasound grand challenge 2024. In: Proceedings of the 27th International Conference on Medical Image Computing and Computer Assisted Intervention (MICCAI 2024). Springer (2024). https://doi.org/10.5281/zenodo.10979813
3. Bai, J., Ou, Z., Lu, Y., Ni, D., Chen, G.: Pubic symphysis-fetal head segmentation from transperineal ultrasound images. In: Proceedings of the International Conference on Medical Image Computing and Computer Assisted Intervention (MICCAI 2023). Springer (2023). https://doi.org/10.5281/zenodo.7861699
4. Bai, J., Sun, Z., Yu, S., Lu, Y., Long, S., Wang, H., Qiu, R., Ou, Z., Zhou, M., Zhi, D., et al.: A framework for computing angle of progression from transperineal ultrasound images for evaluating fetal head descent using a novel double branch network. Front. Physiol. **13**, 940150 (2022)
5. Bai, J., Yang, Z., Hasan, K., Gan, J., Liang, Z., Cai, W., Tan, T., Ye, J., Yaqub, M., Ni, D., Slimani, S., Ohene-Botwe, B., Roman Victor Manuel, C., Lekadir, K.: Fetal ultrasound grand challenge: semi-supervised cervical segmentation (FUGC25). In: Proceedings of the IEEE International Symposium on Biomedical Imaging (ISBI 2025). IEEE (2024). https://doi.org/10.5281/zenodo.14328192

6. Bai, J., Zhou, Z., Ou, Z., Koehler, G., Stock, R., Maier-Hein, K., Elbatel, M., Martí, R., Li, X., Qiu, Y., et al.: PSFHS challenge report: pubic symphysis and fetal head segmentation from intrapartum ultrasound images. Med. Image Anal. **99**, 103353 (2025)

7. Chen, G., Bai, J., Ou, Z., Lu, Y., Wang, H.: PSFHS: intrapartum ultrasound image dataset for AI-based segmentation of pubic symphysis and fetal head. Sci. Data **11**(1), 436 (2024)

8. Chen, J., Lu, Y., Yu, Q., Luo, X., Adeli, E., Wang, Y., Lu, L., Yuille, A.L., Zhou, Y.: Transunet: transformers make strong encoders for medical image segmentation. arXiv preprint arXiv:2102.04306 (2021)

9. Chen, Z., Lu, Y., Long, S., Campello, V.M., Bai, J., Lekadir, K.: Fetal head and pubic symphysis segmentation in intrapartum ultrasound image using a dual-path boundary-guided residual network. IEEE J. Biomed. Health Inform. **28**(8), 4648–4659 (2024)

10. Chen, Z., Ou, Z., Lu, Y., Bai, J.: Direction-guided and multi-scale feature screening for fetal head-pubic symphysis segmentation and angle of progression calculation. Expert Syst. Appl. **245**, 123096 (2024)

11. Jiang, J., Wang, H., Bai, J., Long, S., Chen, S., Campello, V.M., Lekadir, K.: Intrapartum ultrasound image segmentation of pubic symphysis and fetal head using dual student-teacher framework with CNN-VIT collaborative learning. In: International Conference on Medical Image Computing and Computer-Assisted Intervention, pp. 448–458. Springer (2024)

12. Lu, Y., Zhi, D., Zhou, M., Lai, F., Chen, G., Ou, Z., Zeng, R., Long, S., Qiu, R., Zhou, M., et al.: Multitask deep neural network for the fully automatic measurement of the angle of progression. Comput. Math. Methods Med. **2022**(1), 5192338 (2022)

13. Lu, Y., Zhou, M., Zhi, D., Zhou, M., Jiang, X., Qiu, R., Ou, Z., Wang, H., Qiu, D., Zhong, M., et al.: The JNU-IFM dataset for segmenting pubic symphysis-fetal head. Data Brief **41**, 107904 (2022)

14. Ou, Z., Bai, J., Chen, Z., Lu, Y., Wang, H., Long, S., Chen, G.: RTSeg-Net: a lightweight network for real-time segmentation of fetal head and pubic symphysis from intrapartum ultrasound images. Comput. Biol. Med. **175**, 108501 (2024)

15. Qiu, R., Zhou, M., Bai, J., Lu, Y., Wang, H.: PSFHSP-Net: an efficient lightweight network for identifying pubic symphysis-fetal head standard plane from intrapartum ultrasound images. Med. Biol. Eng. Comput. **62**(10), 2975–2986 (2024)

16. Ronneberger, O., Fischer, P., Brox, T.: U-net: convolutional networks for biomedical image segmentation. In: International Conference on Medical Image Computing and Computer-Assisted Intervention, pp. 234–241 (2015)

17. Zhou, Z., Lu, Y., Bai, J., Campello, V.M., Feng, F., Lekadir, K.: Segment anything model for fetal head-pubic symphysis segmentation in intrapartum ultrasound image analysis. Expert Syst. Appl. **263**, 125699 (2025)

A Two-Stage Semi-supervised Ensemble Framework for Automated Angle of Progression Measurement in Intrapartum Ultrasound

Bo Deng[(⊠)], Yu Chen, and Zilun Peng

College of Information Science and Technology, Jinan University,
Guangzhou 510632, China
db0725@stu2024.jnu.edu.cn

Abstract. Accurate and reproducible measurement of the Angle of Progression (AoP) from intrapartum ultrasound is critical for modern labor management, yet manual annotation is hindered by significant intra- and inter-observer variability and workflow inefficiencies. To address this, we propose a fully automated, two-stage deep learning pipeline for precise landmark localization. The first stage employs a multi-model ensemble of U-Net architectures with diverse backbones (EfficientNet-B4 and -B7), trained under a Mean Teacher semi-supervised framework to leverage both labeled and unlabeled data. This stage generates a robust coarse prediction by performing a per-keypoint weighted average of the fused heatmaps. In the second stage, a dedicated Res-Net-18-based regression model refines the position of each landmark by predicting a precise offset from its coarse location on a localized image patch. Our integrated approach, trained on a combined dataset from the 2024 and 2025 IUGC challenges, demonstrates highly competitive performance, achieving a Mean Radial Error (MRE) of 12.7888 pixels and a mean Absolute Parameter Difference (APD) of 4.4581 degrees for the AoP on the test set. This automated framework promises to enhance diagnostic consistency and streamline clinical workflows, aligning with the WHO's vision for improved intrapartum care.

Keywords: Intrapartum Ultrasound · Angle of Progression (AoP) · Two-Stage Model · Semi-Supervised Learning

1 Introduction

Effective intrapartum care, crucial for maternal and fetal well-being, relies on accurate labor monitoring. The World Health Organization (WHO) has recently advanced this effort with its Labour Care Guide (LCG) [10], which promotes standardized, evidence-based assessment. Within this framework, intrapartum ultrasound is an indispensable tool for evaluating fetal head progression, a rec-ommendation strongly supported by the International Society of Ultrasound in

Obstetrics and Gynecology (ISUOG) [4]. A cornerstone of modern ultrasound-based labor assessment is the measurement of the Angle of Progression (AoP), a key biometric calculated from three anatomical landmarks: two points on the pubic symphysis (PS1, PS2) and a point on the fetal head (FH1). The AoP provides critical, quantitative insight into the fetal head's descent through the birth canal, directly informing clinical decisions regarding the mode of delivery and the timing of interventions.

Despite its clinical utility, the manual annotation required to measure AoP presents a significant bottleneck in busy clinical settings. This process is not only time-consuming but also highly dependent on the operator's experience, suffering from substantial intra- and inter-observer variability that compromises its reliability and reproducibility [8]. This challenge underscores an urgent need for an automated, standardized solution that can provide objective and consistent AoP measurements.

To achieve such automation, deep learning (DL) has become the mainstream approach for landmark localization in medical imaging. While initial DL methods based on direct heatmap regression have shown promise [9,12], they often suffer from sensitivity to image quality variations and struggle with large coordinate ranges. In response, more sophisticated coarse-to-fine and cascaded regression strategies were developed to decompose the localization task into more manageable steps, thereby improving precision [3]. However, a key limitation persists across these advanced methods: they are typically supervised and thus fail to leverage the vast amounts of unlabeled data common in the medical domain. The framework proposed in this paper is designed specifically to address this limitation. The key contributions are as follows.

1. We introduce a robust two-stage, coarse-to-fine pipeline that synergistically combines the global context awareness of a first-stage model with the high-precision local analysis of specialized second-stage models.
2. We are the first to apply a multi-model, semi-supervised ensemble for the coarse localization stage. By integrating two U-Net models with diverse EfficientNet backbones [15] and training them within a Mean Teacher framework [16], our method effectively utilizes both labeled and thousands of unlabeled images to enhance generalization and robustness.
3. We demonstrate the efficacy of our complete pipeline through extensive experiments on a large-scale, combined dataset from the 2024 and 2025 IUGC challenges, achieving state-of-the-art performance.
4. The proposed automated framework offers a practical and powerful solution for standardizing AoP measurement, presenting a significant step towards the technical implementation of the WHO's LCG and the broader biomedical objective of safer intrapartum care.

The remainder of this paper is organized as follows. Section 2 reviews related work in landmark localization and semi-supervised learning. Section 3 details our proposed two-stage methodology. Section 4 presents our experimental setup and results, including comprehensive ablation studies. Finally, Sect. 5 concludes the paper and discusses future work.

2   Related Work

This section reviews the key areas of research that form the foundation of our work: deep learning-based landmark localization, semi-supervised learning in medical imaging, and advanced strategies for improving localization accuracy.

2.1   Deep Learning for Landmark Localization

Automated landmark localization is a fundamental task in medical image analysis. Traditional machine learning methods have largely been superseded by deep learning approaches, which have demonstrated superior performance. The dominant paradigm for this task is heatmap regression [9]. In this approach, instead of directly regressing the coordinates of a landmark, the network is trained to predict a 2D Gaussian-like heatmap for each keypoint, where the peak of the heatmap corresponds to the landmark's location. This method provides richer supervision and has been shown to be more robust to initialization and optimization challenges than direct coordinate regression. Seminal works, such as the Stacked Hourglass network [9] for human pose estimation, established the efficacy of this approach. Subsequently, architectures like U-Net [12], originally designed for segmentation, have been widely adapted for heatmap regression in medical imaging due to their powerful encoder-decoder structure and effective use of skip connections to preserve spatial details. While U-Net [12] remains a strong baseline, recent architectures such as TransUNet [1] have started incorporating Transformers to better capture long-range dependencies. To bridge the gap between heatmaps and coordinates, methods like Integral Pose Regression [14] have also proposed differentiable operations for end-to-end training. Nevertheless, these methods are primarily supervised and their performance is tied to the quantity of annotated data.

2.2   Semi-supervised Learning in Medical Imaging

The acquisition of large, expertly annotated medical datasets is a significant bottleneck. Semi-supervised learning (SSL) offers a compelling solution by enabling models to learn from a small set of labeled data alongside a much larger set of unlabeled data. Consistency regularization has emerged as a leading SSL strategy. The core idea is that a model's prediction should remain stable (consistent) under different perturbations of its input or its own parameters. The Mean Teacher framework [16] is a state-of-the-art consistency-based method that has shown great success in medical imaging [17]. It maintains two models: a student model, which is trained via standard backpropagation, and a teacher model, whose weights are an exponential moving average (EMA) of the student's weights. The student is then encouraged to produce predictions consistent with those of the more stable teacher model on unlabeled data, typically by minimizing the Mean Squared Error (MSE) between their outputs. This EMA-based approach provides a more stable pseudo-labeling target than self-ensembling methods. Building upon this, recent approaches like FixMatch [13] have further simplified the SSL framework. Moreover, the inherent robustness of consistency-based methods makes them well-suited for medical data, which often suffers from noisy labels [18], a challenge implicitly addressed by our Mean Teacher approach.

2.3   Advanced Strategies for High-Precision Localization

To push the performance boundaries of landmark localization, several advanced strategies have been proposed. One powerful paradigm is the coarse-to-fine, or two-stage, approach. This strategy decomposes the difficult task of global localization into two simpler steps: first, a coarse prediction to identify the general region of interest, and second, a refined prediction within that localized region. This cascaded approach, rooted in early works on pose regression [3], effectively manages large coordinate ranges and allows a specialized refinement model to focus on local details, leading to higher precision [15]. Another widely adopted technique for enhancing model robustness and accuracy is ensembling. By combining predictions from multiple diverse models, the variance of the individual models' errors can be reduced. A common and effective ensemble strategy involves training models with the same architecture but different backbones [2], such as EfficientNet-B4 and -B7 [15]. Fusing their predictions, for instance by averaging their output heatmaps, often yields a more reliable result than any single model could achieve alone. Our work integrates both of these advanced strategies into a unified, semi-supervised framework.

3   Methodology

To achieve accurate and fully automated measurement of the Angle of Progression (AoP), we propose a novel two-stage, semi-supervised ensemble framework, illustrated in Fig. 1. Our pipeline is divided into two main stages: Semi-Supervised Ensemble Coarse Localization and Local Offset Refinement. In the first stage, an ensemble of models processes the full ultrasound image to generate a Fused Heatmap, from which initial Coarse Coordinates (P) are extracted. Subsequently, in the second stage, specialized refinement networks analyze local image patches (C) centered at these coarse predictions to regress precise Coordinate Offsets (δ). These offsets are then added to the coarse coordinates to produce the final Refined Coordinates (R). The following subsections detail each component of this pipeline.

3.1   Semi-supervised Ensemble Coarse Localization

Network Architecture. Our coarse localization models are built upon the U-Net architecture [12], a fully convolutional network renowned for its efficacy in biomedical image analysis. The U-Net consists of a contracting path (encoder) to capture context and a symmetric expanding path (decoder) to enable precise localization. To further enhance the feature extraction capabilities of our models,

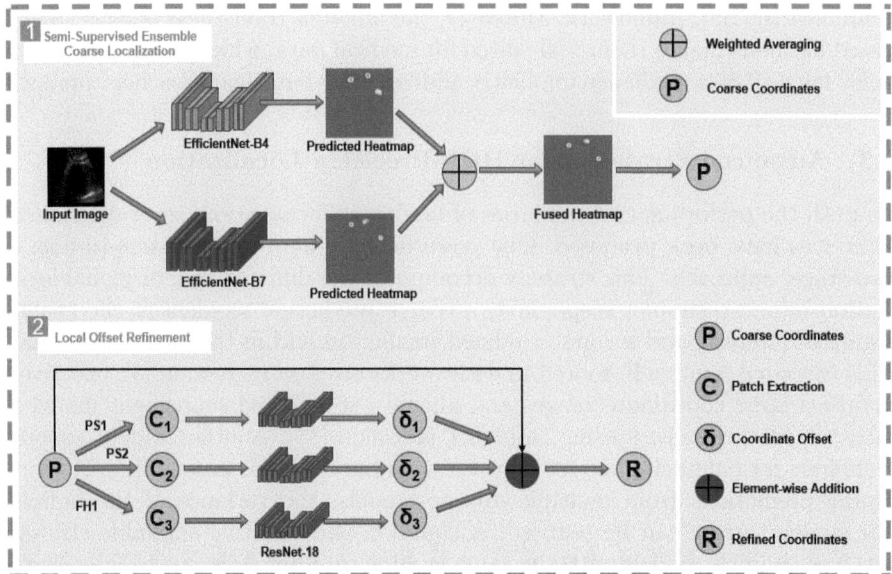

Fig. 1. Overview of our proposed two-stage framework for automated landmark localization.

we employ powerful backbones from the EfficientNet family [15], which are pre-trained on the ImageNet dataset. To foster model diversity, a critical component for effective ensembling, we trained two independent U-Net models utilizing EfficientNet-B4 and EfficientNet-B7 as their respective encoders. Each model outputs a 3-channel heatmap of size 128×128, where each channel corresponds to one of the three target landmarks (PS1, PS2, FH1).

Semi-supervised Training with Mean Teacher. To effectively utilize the large volume of available unlabeled data, each U-Net model was trained within the Mean Teacher semi-supervised framework [16]. This framework consists of two identical models: a student model and a teacher model. The student model, with weights θ_t at training step t, is updated using standard backpropagation. The teacher model, with weights θ'_t, is not trained directly via backpropagation; instead, its weights are updated as an Exponential Moving Average (EMA) of the student's weights:

$$\theta'_t = \alpha\theta'_{t-1} + (1 - \alpha)\theta_t,$$

where α is a smoothing coefficient, or EMA decay rate. This EMA update makes the teacher model a more stable and reliable ensemble of the student's own past states.

The total loss function L for the student model is a combination of a supervised loss L_{sup} on labeled data and an unsupervised consistency loss L_{unsup} on unlabeled data:

$$L = L_{\mathrm{sup}} + w(t) \cdot L_{\mathrm{unsup}}.$$

where $w(t)$ is a time-dependent weighting factor that balances the two losses.

The supervised loss L_{sup} is a Weighted MSE applied to the labeled batch, designed to focus the model on the keypoint peaks. It is defined as:

$$L_{\text{sup}} = \frac{1}{N} \sum_{i=1}^{N} (H_{gl}^{(i)})^{\gamma} \cdot (H_{pred}^{(i)} - H_{gl}^{(i)})^2.$$

where H_{pred} and H_{gl} are the predicted and ground-truth heatmaps, respectively, and γ is a focusing parameter (set to 2 in our experiments).

The consistency L_{unsup} enforces that the student model's prediction on a strongly-augmented unlabeled image, denoted as $f(x'_{u,j}, \theta_t)$, should be consistent with the more stable teacher model's prediction on a weakly-augmented version of the same image, $f(x_{u,j}, \theta'_t)$. The loss is calculated as the MSE between the two outputs, but only for pseudo-labels where the teacher's confidence is high (i.e., the maximum value of the teacher's heatmap exceeds a threshold τ):

$$L_{\text{unsup}} = \frac{1}{M} \sum_{j=1}^{M} M_j \cdot \| f(x'_{u,j}, \theta_t) - f(x_{u,j}, \theta'_t) \|_2^2.$$

where M_j is a mask that is 1 if $\max(\mathcal{T}(f(x_{u,j}, \theta'_t))) \geq \tau$ and 0 otherwise.

The consistency weight $w(t)$ is gradually increased during training using a sigmoid ramp-up function to allow the model to learn from labeled data first before introducing the unsupervised signal.

Ensemble Strategy for Inference. During inference, we leverage the diversity of the two trained models to produce a single, highly robust prediction. For a given input image I, we obtain the predicted heatmaps H_{B4} from the EfficientNet-B4 model and H_{B7} from the EfficientNet-B7 model. The final fused heatmap, H_{fused}, is generated by a per-keypoint weighted average of these two heatmaps:

$$H_{\text{fused},k} = w_{B4,k} \cdot H_{B4,k} + w_{B7,k} \cdot H_{B7,k}.$$

where $k \in \{PS1, PS2, FH1\}$ denotes the keypoint channel, and the weights $w_{B4,k}$ and $w_{B7,k}$ are hyperparameters determined based on the individual performance of each model on the validation set for that specific keypoint. This strategy allows us to capitalize on the strengths of each model for each landmark, resulting in a superior coarse localization.

3.2   Local Offset Refinement

While the first stage provides a robust global localization, its output resolution may not be sufficient for achieving the highest possible precision, which is critical for accurate AoP calculation. To address this, we introduce a second refinement stage that operates on high-resolution local patches, a strategy proven effective in high-precision localization tasks [3,15]. This coarse-to-fine approach allows a specialized model to focus on fine-grained local details without being distracted by the complexity of the entire image.

Patch Extraction. For each of the three landmarks (PS1, PS2, and FH1), we use its coarse coordinate (x_c, y_c), predicted by the ensemble model in Stage 1, as a center point. A high-resolution image patch is then cropped from the original, full-resolution ultrasound image, centered at (x_c, y_c). To handle cases where the coarse prediction is near the image border, we employ zero-padding to ensure that all extracted patches have a consistent, predefined size. Based on our experiments, a patch size of 128×128 pixels was found to provide a robust balance between local detail and sufficient context for all three landmarks.

Refinement Network Architecture. Our refinement network is designed to be lightweight yet powerful enough for the local regression task. We employ a ResNet-18 architecture [5], pre-trained on ImageNet, as the feature extractor. We removed the final average pooling and fully-connected classification layers from the standard ResNet-18. In their place, we appended a custom Multi-Layer Perceptron (MLP) regression head. This head consists of a global average pooling layer, a fully-connected layer with 256 neurons and ReLU activation, a Dropout layer with a rate of 0.5 for regularization, and a final fully-connected layer that outputs a 2-dimensional vector representing the predicted offset.

Learning Objective and Loss Function. The objective of each refinement network is to learn a mapping from an input image patch P to a precise coordinate offset vector $(\Delta x, \Delta y)$. This offset represents the displacement from the coarse prediction (x_c, y_c) to the ground-truth landmark position $(x_g t, y_g t)$. To make the learning target independent of the patch size, the ground-truth offset is normalized by the patch dimension S_{patch}:

$$
\text{label} = \left(\frac{x_{\text{gt}} - x_c}{S_{\text{patch}}}, \frac{y_{\text{gt}} - y_c}{S_{\text{patch}}} \right).
$$

The network is trained to minimize the MSE between its predicted normalized offset and the ground-truth label. This loss function effectively penalizes deviations in the predicted offset, driving the model to learn a highly accurate local correction. We trained a separate, specialized refinement model for each of the three landmarks, allowing each model to learn the specific local features associated with its target.

4   Experiments and Results

To validate the efficacy of our proposed framework, we conducted a series of comprehensive experiments. This section is structured as follows: First, we describe the datasets, evaluation metrics, and our implementation details. Second, we present a thorough ablation study to dissect the individual contribution of each component within our pipeline—namely, semi-supervised learning, model ensembling, and the two-stage refinement. Finally, we report the performance of our complete, optimized model on the official IUGC 2025 test set and compare it against the provided baseline to demonstrate its state-of-the-art capabilities.

4.1   Dataset and Evaluation Metrics

Datasets. The datasets used in our experiments were constructed from the official data of the 2024 and 2025 IUGC challenges. The labeled dataset for our study was formed by combining the labeled sets from both challenges, resulting in a total of 2875 images with corresponding ground-truth coordinates for the three landmarks (PS1, PS2, and FH1). From this combined labeled set, we performed a fixed, stratified split, allocating 2500 images for training and reserving the remaining 375 images as our validation set for hyperparameter tuning and model selection. Additionally, we utilized 4787 unlabeled images from the 2025 IUGC challenge for consistency regularization within our semi-supervised framework.

Evaluation Metrics. We use two primary metrics to assess model performance. The Mean Radial Error (MRE), also known as the mean point distance, calculates the average Euclidean distance in pixels between the predicted and ground-truth coordinates, providing a direct measure of localization accuracy. The APD measures the mean absolute error in degrees between the Angle of Progression (AoP) calculated from the predicted landmarks and that from the ground-truth landmarks. APD evaluates the clinical utility of the predictions by quantifying the accuracy of the derived geometric parameter.

4.2   Implementation Details

All models were implemented within the PyTorch framework and trained on NVIDIA A100 or RTX 4090 GPUs. All input images were preprocessed by resizing to 512×512, followed by Contrast Limited Adaptive Histogram Equalization (CLAHE) [11] to enhance local image contrast.

For the first-stage semi-supervised training, we utilized the AdamW optimizer [7], which decouples weight decay regularization from the adaptive learning rate update, often leading to better generalization. The initial learning rate was set to 1e-4. The teacher model's EMA decay rate, α, was set to 0.999. The maximum consistency weight, w_{max}, was set to 2.0 and was gradually increased over a ramp-up period of 40 epochs. The batch size was 8 for both labeled and unlabeled data.

For the second-stage refinement, we also employed the AdamW optimizer with an initial learning rate of 1e-4. The batch size was set to 64, and the patch size for all three landmarks was 128x128 pixels. For all training processes, we utilized a Cosine Annealing learning rate schedule [6] with a 10-epoch warm-up period to ensure smooth and stable convergence.

4.3   Quantitative Analysis

We now present the quantitative results of our experiments. First, we conduct a detailed ablation study to dissect the contribution of each component in our framework. Then, we compare the final performance of our full pipeline against the official challenge baseline on the test set.

Table 1. Ablation study of framework components on the IUGC 2025 validation set.

Method			Performance Metrics	
EfficientNet-B7	EfficientNet-B4	Refinement Stage	MRE (pixels) ↓	APD (degrees)↓
✓			9.8987	3.7632
	✓		8.5412	2.6852
✓	✓		8.2530	2.5839
✓	✓	✓	**7.9163**	**2.4559**

Ablation Studies. We performed a comprehensive ablation study on the IUGC 2025 validation set to validate each component of our framework. The results are summarized in Table 1.

Our analysis begins with the individual models. The U-Net with an EfficientNet-B4 backbone, trained under our full semi-supervised (SSL) framework, achieved a strong baseline performance with an MRE of 8.5412 pixels. In contrast, the larger EfficientNet-B7 model, trained only on supervised data, performed worse, as expected due to the smaller training set.

Intriguingly, ensembling these two diverse models yielded a result superior to either standalone model. The ensemble lowered the MRE to 8.2530 and the APD to 2.5839. This highlights a key benefit of ensembling heterogeneous models: the diversity in their training schemes (semi-supervised vs. supervised) and architectures created complementary error patterns. The supervised B7 model, though less accurate overall, acted as a regularizer, correcting specific failure modes of the more powerful but potentially biased SSL-trained B4 model.

Finally, the addition of our Refinement Stage provided the most significant performance gain, reducing the MRE to 7.9163 pixels and APD to 2.4559 degrees. This confirms that our full two-stage ensemble pipeline is highly effective, with each component providing a distinct and crucial contribution.

Table 2. Final performance comparison with the official baseline on the IUGC 2025 test set.

Method	MRE (pixels) ↓	APD (degrees)↓
Baseline	21.8273	8.3727
Ours	12.7888	4.4581

Comparison with Official Baseline. To provide a final, unbiased evaluation of our complete framework, we submitted our best-performing model—the full two-stage ensemble with refinement—to the official challenge evaluation server for assessment on the test set. We compare our final results against the official baseline provided by the IUGC 2025 challenge organizers. As shown in Table 2, our method achieves a dramatic improvement over the baseline across both key metrics. Our final model obtained an MRE of 12.7888 pixels and an APD of 4.4581 degrees on the test set. Compared to the official baseline's performance of 21.83 pixels MRE and 8.37 degrees APD, our framework achieved a remarkable 41.4% reduction in MRE and a 46.8% reduction in APD. This substantial improvement in a challenging, unseen dataset underscores the real-world efficacy and strong generalization capability of our integrated semi-supervised, ensemble, and two-stage refinement approach.

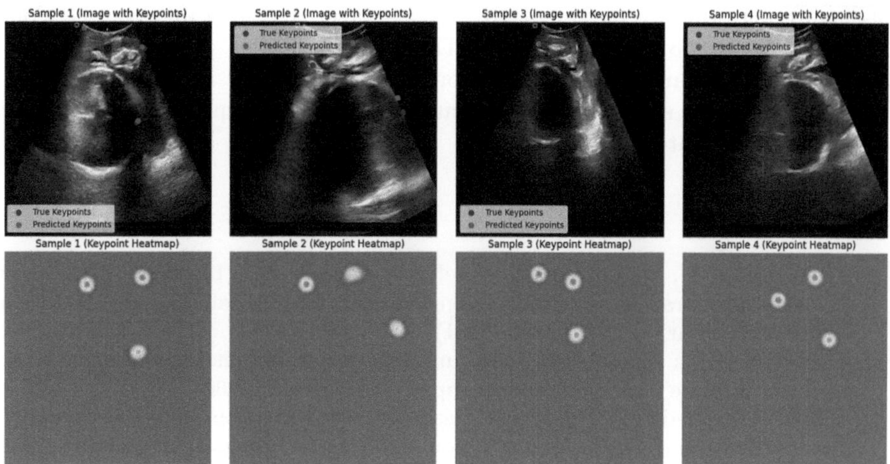

Fig. 2. Qualitative visualization of our model's predictions on four randomly selected samples from the training set.

4.4   Qualitative Analysis

In addition to the quantitative metrics, we provide qualitative visualizations to offer further insight into our model's behavior. Fig. 2 displays the prediction results on four randomly selected samples from our combined training set. In most cases (Samples 1, 3, and 4), our full pipeline demonstrates excellent performance, accurately localizing all three landmarks with high precision.

Sample 2 illustrates a more challenging scenario. While the pubic symphysis landmarks (PS1 and PS2) are still accurately identified, the prediction for the Fetal Head (FH1) landmark shows a noticeable deviation from the ground truth. The corresponding heatmap for FH1 appears more diffuse and less confident compared to the other landmarks. This type of failure case typically occurs in images with low contrast or ambiguous anatomical features for the fetal head, highlighting a potential area for future improvement, such as incorporating more advanced context-aware mechanisms. Overall, the visualizations confirm the strong performance of our method on the majority of samples.

5   Conclusion

In this work, we proposed a novel two-stage, semi-supervised ensemble framework to address the critical challenge of automated Angle of Progression (AoP) measurement in intrapartum ultrasound. By synergistically combining a powerful semi-supervised, multi-model ensemble for coarse localization with specialized, high-resolution refinement models, our pipeline robustly handles the complexities of clinical ultrasound data. Extensive ablation studies validated the significant contribution of each component. Our final model achieves state-of-the-art performance on the IUGC 2025 test set, reaching an Average Point Distance of 12.7888 pixels and an APD of 4.4581 degrees. This work presents a highly effective and practical solution for standardizing intrapartum assessment, representing a tangible step towards enhancing the quality and efficiency of modern labor care.

References

1. Chen, J., Lu, Y., Yu, Q., Luo, X., Adeli, E., Wang, Y., Lu, L., Yuille, A.L., Zhou, Y.: Transunet: transformers make strong encoders for medical image segmentation. arXiv preprint arXiv:2102.04306 (2021)
2. Dietterich, T.G.: Ensemble methods in machine learning. In: International Workshop on Multiple Classifier Systems, pp. 1–15. Springer (2000)
3. Dollár, P., Welinder, P., Perona, P.: Cascaded pose regression. In: IEEE Computer Society Conference on Computer Vision and Pattern Recognition, pp. 1078–1085. IEEE (2010)
4. Ghi, T., Eggebø, T., Lees, C., Kalache, K., Rozenberg, P., Youssef, A., Salomon, L., Tutschek, B.: ISUOG practice guidelines: intrapartum ultrasound. Ultrasound Obstet. Gynecol. **52**(1), 128–139 (2018)
5. He, K., Zhang, X., Ren, S., Sun, J.: Deep residual learning for image recognition. In: Proceedings of the IEEE Conference on Computer Vision and Pattern Recognition, pp. 770–778 (2016)
6. Loshchilov, I., Hutter, F.: SGDR: stochastic gradient descent with warm restarts. arXiv preprint arXiv:1608.03983 (2016)
7. Loshchilov, I., Hutter, F.: Decoupled weight decay regularization. arXiv preprint arXiv:1711.05101 (2017)
8. Nassr, A.A., Hessami, K., Berghella, V., Bibbo, C., Shamshirsaz, A.A., Shirdel Abdolmaleki, A., Marsoosi, V., Clark, S.L., Belfort, M.A., Shamshirsaz, A.A.: Angle of progression measured using transperineal ultrasound for prediction of uncomplicated operative vaginal delivery: systematic review and meta-analysis. Ultrasound Obstet. Gynecol. **60**(3), 338–345 (2022). https://doi.org/10.1002/uog.24886
9. Newell, A., Yang, K., Deng, J.: Stacked hourglass networks for human pose estimation. In: European Conference on Computer Vision, pp. 483–499. Springer (2016)
10. World Health Organization: Who labour care guide: user's manual. In: WHO labour care guide: user's manual (2020)
11. Pizer, S.M., Amburn, E.P., Austin, J.D., Cromartie, R., Geselowitz, A., Greer, T., ter Haar Romeny, B., Zimmerman, J.B., Zuiderveld, K.: Adaptive histogram equalization and its variations. Comput. Vis. Graph. Image Process. **39**(3), 355–368 (1987)

12. Ronneberger, O., Fischer, P., Brox, T.: U-net: convolutional networks for biomedical image segmentation. In: International Conference on Medical Image Computing and Computer-Assisted Intervention, pp. 234–241. Springer (2015)
13. Sohn, K., Berthelot, D., Carlini, N., Zhang, Z., Zhang, H., Raffel, C.A., Cubuk, E.D., Kurakin, A., Li, C.L.: Fixmatch: simplifying semi-supervised learning with consistency and confidence. Adv. Neural. Inf. Process. Syst. **33**, 596–608 (2020)
14. Sun, X., Xiao, B., Wei, F., Liang, S., Wei, Y.: Integral human pose regression. In: Proceedings of the European Conference on Computer Vision (ECCV), pp. 529–545 (2018)
15. Tan, M., Le, Q.: Efficientnet: rethinking model scaling for convolutional neural networks. In: International Conference on Machine Learning, pp. 6105–6114. PMLR (2019)
16. Tarvainen, A., Valpola, H.: Mean teachers are better role models: Weight-averaged consistency targets improve semi-supervised deep learning results. Adv. Neural Inf. Process. Syst. **30** (2017)
17. Van Engelen, J.E., Hoos, H.H.: A survey on semi-supervised learning. Mach. Learn. **109**(2), 373–440 (2020)
18. Yao, Y., Sun, Z., Zhang, C., Shen, F., Wu, Q., Zhang, J., Tang, Z.: Jo-src: A contrastive approach for combating noisy labels. In: Proceedings of the IEEE/CVF Conference on Computer Vision and Pattern Recognition, pp. 5192–5201 (2021)

GRM Framework

Saeid Rezaei[✉]

University College Cork, Cork, Ireland
`saeid.rezaei@ucc.ie`

Abstract. The standardization of intrapartum care, as promoted by the World Health Organization's Labour Care Guide (LCG), relies on the consistent monitoring of maternal and fetal well-being. A critical component of this process is the assessment of fetal head progression using intrapartum ultrasound, specifically by measuring the Angle of Progression (AoP). However, manual landmark annotation for AoP calculation is time-consuming and prone to inter-observer variability, creating a bottleneck in clinical workflows. To address this, we propose an automated approach for fetal biometry. The core challenge in developing such a deep learning-based solution is the complex and computationally expensive task of optimizing neural network architecture and hyperparameters. In this work, we introduce a novel framework based on a Generative Reward Machine (GRM) to create an autonomous agent that intelligently and efficiently navigates the joint space of batch size and hyperparameters. This method accelerates the development of robust models for automated landmark detection, aiming to enhance diagnostic consistency and support the implementation of safer, evidence-based intrapartum care.

Keywords: Intrapartum Ultrasound · Angle of Progression · Automated Landmark Detection · Generative Reward Machine · Hyperparameter Optimization

1 Introduction

Labor is a dynamic process that requires continuous monitoring to ensure the safety of both mother and fetus. In 2018, the World Health Organization (WHO) published 56 recommendations to improve intrapartum care and promote respectful, woman-centered childbirth experiences. Building on these guidelines, the WHO introduced the Labour Care Guide (LCG) in 2020—a next-generation tool designed to standardize evidence-based labor monitoring through systematic recording of maternal/fetal well-being and prompt identification of labor deviations. Among the critical aspects of labor management supported by the LCG, the evaluation of fetal head position and progression plays a pivotal role in guiding timely clinical decisions. In busy clinical settings, immediate access to reliable diagnostic tools such as intrapartum ultrasound is essential, particularly when labor delay is suspected or prior to instrumental delivery, as recommended by the International Society of Ultrasound in Obstetrics and Gynecology.

J. Bai et al. (Eds.): IUGC 2025, LNCS 16317, pp. 100–104, 2026.
https://doi.org/10.1007/978-3-032-11616-1_9

A cornerstone of ultrasound-based labor assessment is the identification of landmarks in intrapartum images, which form the basis for calculating key parameters like the angle of progression (AoP). The AoP provides critical insight into fetal head descent and rotation during labor and directly influences decisions about interventions. However, obtaining consistent landmark annotations remains a major challenge: current workflows require time-consuming manual analysis by experienced obstetricians, and intra-/inter-observer variability compromises measurement reliability. This bottleneck highlights the urgent need for automated solutions to standardize intrapartum assessments and align with the LCG's goal of enhancing care quality.

To address this need, the challenge tasks participants with developing a fully automated fetal biometry method. The solution should identify three key anatomical landmarks in intrapartum ultrasound images and get the AoP. Successful methods could significantly reduce clinical workflow burdens and improve diagnostic consistency—advancing both the technical implementation of the WHO's LCG framework and the biomedical objective of safer, more equitable intrapartum care worldwide.

1.1   Angle of Progression (AoP)

The following figure illustrates the main process of measuring AoP. To measure the Angle of Progression (AoP), first identify the two farthest points (PS1 and PS2) along the pubic symphysis (PS) contour. Then, draw a tangent line from the rightmost point (PS1) that just touches the fetal head (FH), marking where it intersects as the third point (FH1). The angle formed by these three points (PS1, PS2, and FH1) is the AoP, which helps assess how far the baby's head has descended during labor.

2   Method

The dual challenge of selecting an optimal neural network batch size and tuning its corresponding hyperparameters represents a significant bottleneck in the deep learning pipeline. Traditional methods using grid search are computationally prohibitive and fail to leverage information gathered during the optimization process. In this work, we implemented a novel framework based on a Generative Reward Machine (GRM) to create an autonomous agent that intelligently navigates the joint space of batch size and hyperparameters.

The Generative Reward Machine concept is a construct for problems where inherently noisy partial observations make a perfect Reward Machine impossible to formulate. An estimator maps observations from the environment to a space of estimated states. Transitions within the reward machine's Finite State Machine are prompted by the observation of transitions within this estimated space; the agent, in turn, learns a policy for action within this same space. The objective is the approximation of a perfect Reward Machine.

In a simple case, the programmer specifies the estimated space, the estimator, and the reward machine. In a more complex case, the learning of these components must occur through interactions with the environment, for example, by inferring a complex neural network encoder to function as the estimator, which creates a mapping to a latent space of estimated states. The GRM agent acquires the capacity to interpret early training dynamics within a batch size-specific context, which facilitates the identification of high-performing configurations and the pruning of unpromising trials. This state-aware, adaptive approach significantly enhances the sample efficiency of the search process, offering a robust solution for automated model selection and optimization.

2.1   The GRM Optimization Framework

This work introduces a framework based on the GRM for the automated and simultaneous selection of a model batch size and its hyperparameters. By decomposing the problem into an offline estimation phase and an online search phase, the framework yields an agent that learns to allocate computational resources efficiently, accelerating the discovery of optimal model-configuration pairs. The proposed framework integrates a reward-estimation phase with a search policy based on reinforcement learning (RL). It comprises two primary stages as detailed in Algorithm 1.

Phase 1: Offline Reward Model Estimation The objective of the first phase is the construction of an "estimator" for every potential class of model batch size. This estimator is trained to predict the final, true performance of a model by utilizing the characteristics of its initial training dynamics. This procedure obviates the requirement for the complete training of every configuration during the search phase. The definition of the state space s for the RL agent is the set of candidate batch size classes. For every class $c \in C$, a dataset is generated through the training of the batch size using a diverse and randomly sampled set of hyperparameter configurations.

Following each complete training run, two key pieces of information are stored: the ground-truth validation performance (P_{true}) and the full training log (L). A feature vector (v) is extracted from each log to provide a numerical representation of the training dynamics (e.g., the rate of loss decrease). Subsequently, a regression model is trained for each batch size class to learn a weight vector W_s that establishes a mapping defined by $P_{\text{true}} \approx W_s \cdot v$.

Phase 2: Online RL-based Hyperparameter and Batch Size Search The second phase involves deploying a Q-learning agent to execute an efficient online search. The agent's objective is to learn an optimal policy, $\pi^*(s, a)$, for selecting the best action a (a hyperparameter vector) for a given state s (a batch size class). Within each episode, the agent utilizes its current Q-table, in conjunction with an ϵ-greedy exploration strategy, to select a batch size s and its corresponding hyperparameters a. The selected model undergoes training for a limited number of epochs, sufficient to produce a partial training log from which a dynamics feature vector, v_{episode}, is extracted.

The crucial step is the reward calculation. The reward signal provided to the agent is defined as reward $= W'_s \cdot v_{\text{episode}}$, where W'_s denotes the specific weight vector learned for that batch size during Phase 1. This process guides the search toward favorable batch size-hyperparameter pairs that exhibit promising early-stage dynamics, significantly reducing computational cost.

Algorithm 1. Generative Reward Machine (GRM) Framework

1: **Phase 1: Offline Reward Model Estimation**
2: Let C be the set of model batch size classes (states).
3: Initialize dataset $D_c \leftarrow \emptyset$ for each class $c \in C$.
4: **for** each batch size class $c \in C$ **do**
5:     **for** $k = 1$ to NUM_SAMPLES **do**
6:         Sample a random hyperparameter configuration a_k.
7:         Train model c with hyperparameters a_k to completion.
8:         Obtain training log L_k and true validation performance $P_{\text{true},k}$.
9:         Extract dynamics feature vector v_k from L_k.
10:        $D_c \leftarrow D_c \cup (v_k, P_{\text{true},k})$.
11:     Train a regression model on D_c to learn weight vector W_c such that $P_{\text{true}} \approx W_c \cdot v$.

12: **Phase 2: Online RL-based Hyperparameter Search**
13: Initialize Q-table $Q(s,a)$ for all states $s \in C$ and actions $a \in A$.
14: **for** episode $= 1$ to MAX_EPISODES **do**
15:     Select a batch size class $s \in C$.
16:     Choose action (hyperparameters) a from $Q(s, \cdot)$ using an exploration strategy.
17:     Train model s with hyperparameters a for a limited number of epochs.
18:     Obtain partial training log L_{episode}.
19:     Extract dynamics feature vector v_{episode} from L_{episode}.
20:     reward $\leftarrow W'_s \cdot v_{\text{episode}}$.
21:     Update $Q(s,a)$ using the calculated reward.
22: **return** The optimal policy $\pi^*(s) = \arg\max_a Q(s,a)$.

---

3 Conclusion

The development of automated tools for intrapartum assessment is crucial for advancing the goals of the WHO's Labour Care Guide and improving maternal-fetal outcomes. This paper addresses the significant challenge of automated fetal biometry from intrapartum ultrasound by focusing on a foundational bottleneck: the efficient optimization of the underlying deep learning models. We introduced a Generative Reward Machine (GRM) framework designed to autonomously and jointly select the optimal batch size and hyperparameters. By learning to predict model performance from early training dynamics, the GRM framework significantly reduces the computational burden associated with traditional tuning methods. This approach not only accelerates the development cycle but also enhances the potential for creating a highly accurate and reliable automated system for AoP measurement. The proposed method represents a key step toward deploying robust clinical decision support tools that can reduce workflow burdens, improve diagnostic consistency, and ultimately contribute to safer childbirth practices worldwide.

References

1. Rezaei, S., Brown, K.N.: Generative reward machine for reinforcement learning for physical internet distribution centre. In: Nicosia, G., Ojha, V., Giesselbach, S., Pardalos, M.P., Umeton, R. (eds.) Machine Learning, Optimization, and Data Science. LOD ACAIN 2024, LNCS, vol. 15508. Springer, Cham (2025). https://doi.org/10.1007/978-3-031-82481-4_22

Heatmap Regression for Automated Angle of Progression Measurement: The Baseline Method for the IUGC2025

Yitong Tang[1], Zihao Zhou[1], Yaosheng Lu[1], Jieyun Bai[1(✉)], Shun Long[1], Yuxin Huang[2], Isaac Khobo[3], Shun Zhang[2], Zimo Zhou[2], and Lei Guo[2]

[1] College of Information Science and Technology, Jinan University, Guangzhou 510632, China
`jbai996@aucklanduni.ac.nz`
[2] Department of Obstetrics and Gynecology, Zhujiang Hospital, Southern Medical University, Guangzhou 510260, China
[3] University of Cape Town, Rondebosch, Cape Town 7701, South Africa

Abstract. Angle of Progression (AoP) is a critical parameter for clinical assessment of fetal head descent and prediction of delivery mode, traditionally measured manually by experienced clinicians, which leads to efficiency and consistency issues. In this paper, we present a heatmap regression-based keypoint detection method as a baseline approach for the Intrapartum Ultrasound Grand Challenge (IUGC) 2025, designed to automatically measure the AoP in intrapartum ultrasound images. We employ a U-Net architecture for heatmap prediction to directly identify the three key points required for AoP measurement, followed by post-processing to extract precise coordinates. The method was evaluated on the IUGC 2025 dataset, trained with 300 annotated samples and tested on 501 samples, achieving an average AoP error of 8.37° and a MRE of 21.83 pixels. As a baseline method, we discuss current limitations and propose improvement directions, including semi-supervised learning to leverage unlabeled data, adoption of more advanced network architectures, and optimization of post-processing techniques. This study demonstrates the feasibility of automated AoP measurement in obstetric ultrasound imaging, potentially improving decision support tools in obstetric clinical practice.

Keywords: Intrapartum Ultrasound · Angle of Progression · Keypoint Detection · Heatmap Regression · U-Net

1 Introduction

The delivery modalities are primarily bifurcated into vaginal delivery and cesarean section [1]. The former respects maternal physiological mechanisms and demonstrates lower morbidity and mortality indices for the maternal-fetal dyad, whereas the latter represents an alternative intervention when maternal

© The Author(s), under exclusive license to Springer Nature Switzerland AG 2026
J. Bai et al. (Eds.): IUGC 2025, LNCS 16317, pp. 105–117, 2026.
https://doi.org/10.1007/978-3-032-11616-1_10

or fetal pathophysiology precludes vaginal parturition [2]. Optimizing maternal and neonatal outcomes through reduction of unnecessary operative interventions while ensuring timely cesarean deliveries necessitates precise assessment of labor progression in contemporary obstetric practice.

Traditional labor monitoring methodologies predominantly utilize digital vaginal examinations, which the World Health Organization advocates performing at 4-hour intervals during the first stage of labor [3]. However, substantial evidence indicates that vaginal assessment of fetal head station and position demonstrates limited accuracy and significant subjectivity, particularly when cephalohematoma impedes palpation of cranial sutures and fontanels [4,5]. Moreover, repeated examinations potentially facilitate ascending microbial migration from the vagina to the cervix and uterus, presenting potential neonatal infectious risks [5].

Intrapartum ultrasonography has emerged as a superior methodological alternative for labor progression evaluation. Multiple investigations have demonstrated that sonographic measurements exhibit enhanced accuracy, objectivity, and reproducibility compared with digital examination [6,7]. Furthermore, ultrasonographic assessment neither elicits patient discomfort nor requires substantial additional clinical time [8]. Among various sonographic parameters,AoP has been identified as the most reproducible parameter for evaluating fetal head descent [9].

The AOP is defined as the angle formed by the two farthest points (PS1 and PS2) along the pubic symphysis contour and the point of tangency (FH1) where a tangent line drawn from the rightmost point (PS1) touches the fetal head .This measurement provides critical information regarding both the current position of the fetal head relative to the ischial spines and the trajectory of labor progression [10]. Research demonstrates that an AoP exceeding 120 degrees correlates significantly with successful spontaneous vaginal delivery probability, establishing it as a valuable predictive indicator of delivery modality [11].

The contemporary AoP measurement paradigm predominantly relies on manual assessments performed by experienced clinicians—a methodology characterized by temporal inefficiency and potential measurement inconsistencies [12]. The development of automated algorithms for AoP quantification therefore presents a significant opportunity to enhance both efficiency and precision in clinical labor assessment protocols. Nevertheless, significant challenges persist in the accurate segmentation of relevant anatomical structures due to inherent ultrasonographic limitations, including speckle noise, attenuation, artifacts, and suboptimal signal-to-noise ratios [13]. Additionally, transperineal ultrasound images frequently exhibit blurred anatomical targets, indistinct contours, and interference from adjacent tissues [14], with fetal head boundaries particularly susceptible to delineation difficulties due to normal sutures, sonographic artifacts, or interference from the similarly echogenic uterine wall [15].

Previous research on automated AoP measurement has primarily adopted segmentation-based methods, which first perform complete segmentation of the pubic symphysis and fetal head contours in ultrasound images, and then calculate AoP based on the segmentation results.

Within these segmentation-based frameworks, the predominant strategy for extracting the keypoints (PS1, PS2, and FH1) involves elliptical modeling of the anatomical structures. Specifically, the segmented contours of the pubic symphysis and fetal head are typically subjected to ellipse fitting algorithms [16–19]. While some implementations perform dual ellipse fitting for both structures to derive the pubic symphysis endpoints (PS1 and PS2) and the fetal head tangent point (FH1) [16,19], others employ a hybrid approach by directly regressing the pubic symphysis endpoints (PS1 and PS2) and applying ellipse fitting only to the fetal head to determine FH1 [17,18]. Despite its widespread adoption, the ellipse fitting process constitutes an additional source of measurement error. This error arises because the anatomical structures may not conform perfectly to elliptical shapes, and the fitting accuracy is highly contingent upon segmentation quality. Moreover, the least-squares fitting algorithms themselves introduce numerical approximations. Consequently, these errors propagate to the subsequent AoP computation, potentially compromising measurement precision. Notably, all existing automated methodologies rely on intermediate segmentation and/or geometric modeling steps, with none directly regressing the three key coordinate points required for AoP computation.

Recent advancements in computational obstetrics have sought to address these segmentation challenges through alternative methodological paradigms. The IUGC 2025 Challenge (hosted at MICCAI) proposes a shift toward keypoint detection-based AoP measurement, departing from conventional segmentation-dependent approaches.This challenge focuses on keypoint detection , which directly identifies the three key coordinate points (PS1, PS2, and FH1) required for AoP measurement to calculate process parameters. The present study provides a comprehensive description of the baseline approach employed in IUGC2025 to enhance participants' comprehension of the methodological details.

2   Method

2.1   Overview of Network

This study employs a heatmap-based regression approach for landmark detection in intrapartum ultrasound images, enabling precise measurement of the AoP. Our methodology addresses the challenge of directly identifying the three critical landmarks (PS1, PS2, and FH1) required for AoP calculation through heatmap prediction and coordinate extraction.

Our approach employs a three-stage pipeline:

- **Label Preprocessing**: During training data loading, ground truth heatmaps are generated by encoding landmark coordinates as Gaussian distributions centered at each keypoint location.
- **Heatmap Prediction**: These heatmaps serve as training targets for a U-Net architecture, which learns to predict pixel-wise likelihood maps for keypoint presence.

- **Coordinate Extraction**: At inference time, predicted heatmaps undergo post-processing to extract precise landmark coordinates.

Figure 1 illustrates the complete workflow of our proposed heatmap-based landmark detection system, which consists of the following key components: label preprocessing based on Gaussian distributions, heatmap prediction via U-Net, coordinate extraction and AoP calculation.

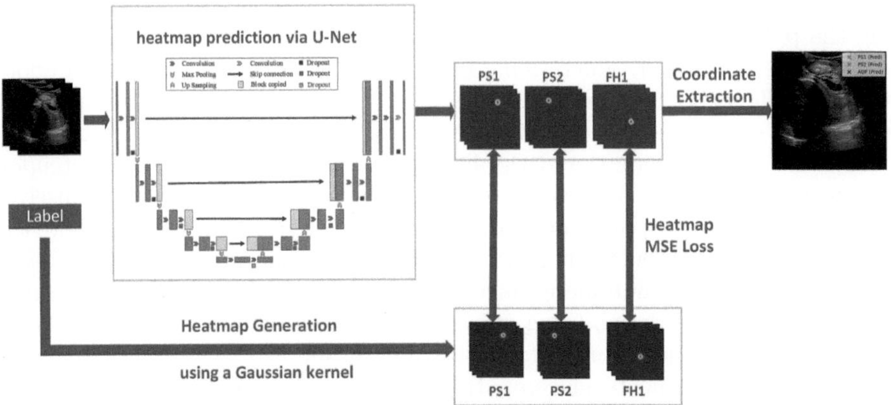

Fig. 1. Workflow of heatmap-based landmark detection system

2.2 Label Preprocessing

The network is trained to predict heatmaps that represent the spatial probability distribution of landmark locations. For each of the three landmarks (PS1, PS2, and FH1), a ground truth heatmap is generated using a Gaussian kernel centered at the annotated landmark coordinates [20].

The ground truth heatmap for each landmark is generated as follows:

$$H(x,y) = \exp\left(-\frac{(x - x_0)^2 + (y - y_0)^2}{2\sigma^2}\right) \tag{1}$$

where (x_0, y_0) represents the ground truth landmark coordinates scaled to the heatmap dimensions, and σ controls the spread of the Gaussian peak. We empirically set $\sigma = 2.0$ to balance between localization precision and network trainability.

The process of generating ground truth heatmaps involves:

1. Normalizing input images to dimensions of 512×512 pixels
2. Scaling annotated landmark coordinates (PS1, PS2, FH1) to match the heatmap dimensions (64×64)

3. Generating a separate Gaussian heatmap for each landmark using Eq. 1
4. Ensuring that heatmap values range between 0 and 1, with the peak value of 1 at the landmark location.

This representation transforms the discrete landmark detection problem into a continuous heatmap regression task, which proves advantageous in handling the inherent noise and ambiguity in ultrasound images. The Gaussian distribution accommodates slight annotation variations and provides a smoother optimization landscape during training.

2.3   Heatmap Prediction

Network Architecture. A fully convolutional U-Net architecture is employed to predict heatmaps. This architecture is specifically designed for generating high-resolution feature maps while preserving spatial information crucial for precise landmark localization.

The network encompasses an encoder-decoder structure with skip connections, comprising four core components: an encoder pathway, a bottleneck, a decoder pathway, and an output layer. This structure facilitates gradient flow and feature reuse throughout the network.

Encoder Pathway: The encoder comprises four sequential blocks. Each block contains two 3×3 convolutional layers with batch normalization and ReLU activation, followed by 2×2 max pooling. The network begins with 64 channels, which double after each pooling operation, reaching 512 channels at the deepest encoder level. This progressive channel expansion enables the extraction of increasingly complex features while reducing spatial dimensions from 512×512 to 32×32.

Bottleneck: The bottleneck serves as a transition between encoder and decoder pathways, consisting of two convolutional layers with 1024 channels that capture the most abstract features with the broadest receptive field.

Decoder Pathway: The decoder mirrors the encoder with four sequential upsampling blocks. Each block begins with a 2×2 transposed convolution that doubles the spatial dimensions while halving the channel count. Features from the corresponding encoder level are concatenated via skip connections, followed by two 3×3 convolutional layers with batch normalization and ReLU activation. This architecture facilitates the gradual recovery of spatial detail while integrating multi-scale contextual information from the encoder.

Output Layer: The final layer consists of a 1×1 convolution that reduces the channel dimension to match the number of keypoints (three in our case), producing three separate heatmap channels corresponding to PS1, PS2, and FH1 landmarks.

The network architecture ensures that the output heatmaps maintain a consistent size of 64×64 pixels, achieving an optimal balance between computational efficiency and localization precision. The architectural parameters are summarized in Table 1.

Table 1. U-Net Architecture for Landmark Heatmap Regression

Layer	Output Size	Parameters
Input	3×512×512	–
Encoder Block 1	64×256×256	Conv(3→64), Conv(64→64), MaxPool
Encoder Block 2	128×128×128	Conv(64→128), Conv(128→128), MaxPool
Encoder Block 3	256×64×64	Conv(128→256), Conv(256→256), MaxPool
Encoder Block 4	512×32×32	Conv(256→512), Conv(512→512), MaxPool
Bottleneck	1024×32×32	Conv(512→1024), Conv(1024→1024)
Decoder Block 4	512×64×64	ConvTranspose(1024→512), Conv(1024→512), Conv(512→512)
Decoder Block 3	256×128×128	ConvTranspose(512→256), Conv(512→256), Conv(256→256)
Decoder Block 2	128×256×256	ConvTranspose(256→128), Conv(256→128), Conv(128→128)
Decoder Block 1	64×512×512	ConvTranspose(128→64), Conv(128→64), Conv(64→64)
Output	3×64×64	Conv(64→3), Resize

Loss Function. We employ Mean Squared Error (MSE) [21] as the primary loss function for training our heatmap regression network. The MSE loss measures the pixel-wise difference between the predicted heatmaps and the ground truth Gaussian heatmaps:

$$\mathcal{L}_{MSE} = \frac{1}{NKP} \sum_{n=1}^{N} \sum_{k=1}^{K} \sum_{p=1}^{P} (H_{n,k,p}^{pred} - H_{n,k,p}^{gt})^2 \tag{2}$$

where N represents the batch size, K denotes the number of landmarks (3 in our case), P is the number of pixels in each heatmap (64×64), $H_{n,k,p}^{pred}$ is the predicted heatmap value, and $H_{n,k,p}^{gt}$ is the ground truth heatmap value for the n-th sample, k-th landmark, and p-th pixel.

MSE loss is particularly suitable for heatmap regression as it penalizes large deviations more severely than small ones, encouraging the network to produce precise peaks at landmark locations. Additionally, it provides a stable gradient flow during training, facilitating convergence even with limited training data.

2.4   Coordinate Extraction

Following heatmap prediction, we extract precise landmark coordinates through post-processing.

Maximum Response Location. The simplest approach identifies the pixel with the maximum value in each heatmap channel:

$$(x^{pred}, y^{pred}) = \arg\max_{(x,y)} H(x, y) \tag{3}$$

where $H(x, y)$ represents the predicted heatmap value at location (x, y). The resulting integer coordinates are then normalized by dividing by the heatmap dimensions to obtain values in the range $[0, 1]$, which can be mapped back to the original image coordinates.

The extracted coordinates for all three landmarks (PS1, PS2, and FH1) are then denormalized to the original image dimensions and used for calculating the AOP.

2.5   Training Details

The network was trained using an Adam optimizer with an initial learning rate of 10^{-4} and weight decay of 10^{-4} to prevent overfitting. We implemented a step learning rate scheduler that reduces the learning rate by a factor of 0.5 every 15 epochs, facilitating convergence in later training stages.

Training was conducted for 150 epochs with a batch size of 4 on standardized ultrasound images resized to 512×512 pixels. Data augmentation techniques were deliberately minimal to preserve the anatomical integrity of the ultrasound images, which is crucial for accurate landmark detection.

To monitor training progress and prevent overfitting, we tracked both the heatmap loss and the coordinate distance metrics. Model checkpoints were saved at regular intervals (every 50 epochs) as well as when achieving the best performance on either the training loss or coordinate distance metrics.

The training process leveraged TensorBoard for real-time visualization of loss curves, learning rates, and sample predictions, enabling continuous assessment of model convergence. Training was conducted on a NVIDIA RTX 2080Ti GPU.

3   Experiments and Results

3.1   Evaluation Metrics

We evaluated our model using several complementary metrics to assess landmark detection accuracy and clinical applicability:

Mean Radial Error (MRE). MRE is adopted as the primary metric, quantifying the average Euclidean distance (in pixels) between predicted landmarks (x_p, y_p) and ground truth landmarks (x_g, y_g) . For each landmark, the radial error R_i is computed as:

$$R_i = \sqrt{(x_p - x_g)^2 + (y_p - y_g)^2} \tag{4}$$

The MRE across N landmarks are then defined as:

$$MRE = \frac{1}{N} \sum_{i=1}^{N} R_i \tag{5}$$

All values are reported in pixel space (range 0–512). Lower MRE values indicate superior localization accuracy.

AOP Error. Given the clinical significance of AoP, we directly calculate the absolute difference between the angles derived from predicted landmarks and ground truth landmarks:

$$\Delta AoP = |AoP^{pred} - AoP^{gt}| \tag{6}$$

The AoP is calculated using the law of cosines:

$$AoP = \cos^{-1}\left(\frac{a^2 + b^2 - c^2}{2ab}\right) \cdot \frac{180}{\pi} \tag{7}$$

where a is the distance between PS1 and PS2, b is the distance between PS1 and FH1, and c is the distance between PS2 and FH1.

Our evaluation protocol provides a comprehensive assessment of model performance, combining pixel-level accuracy with clinically relevant angular measurements to ensure that the proposed method meets both technical and practical requirements for automated AoP determination in clinical settings.

3.2   Datasets

The IUGC2025 challenge dataset comprises 31,421 intrapartum ultrasound images collected from multiple clinical centers, with the following official division:

- Training set: 31,421 cases (including 300 annotated samples with landmark coordinates)
- Validation set: 100 fully annotated cases
- Test set: 501 fully annotated cases.

Our baseline method utilizes only the labeled portion of the training data (300 annotated samples) for supervised learning, intentionally excluding unlabeled data to establish a fundamental performance benchmark.

This experimental design intentionally limits the baseline model to supervised learning from scarce annotated data, demonstrating the fundamental feasibility of landmark detection while highlighting potential improvements through semi-supervised approaches that could leverage the substantial unlabeled data.

3.3   Results

The proposed methodology was evaluated on the official IUGC2025 challenge dataset comprising 601 annotated intrapartum ultrasound images, with 100 samples allocated for validation and 501 for testing. All experiments were conducted under standardized conditions using a single NVIDIA RTX 2080Ti GPU, ensuring consistency in computational resources and environmental parameters. We evaluated the proposed heatmap-based landmark detection model on the provided validation and test datasets.

Table 2. Comprehensive evaluation metrics on validation and test sets.

Metric	Validation (N=100)	Test (N=501)
PS1 MRE (pixels)	12.3408	10.6720
PS2 MRE (pixels)	21.5383	15.6234
FH1 MRE (pixels)	48.1807	39.1866
MRE of all landmarks (pixels)	27.35	21.83
coordinates MAE(pixels)	16.8517	14.0043
Mean AoP Error (°)	10.47	8.37

Quantitative Results. Table 2 presents the comprehensive evaluation metrics for both validation and test sets. The model demonstrates robust performance across all metrics, with particularly notable results in clinical AoP measurement accuracy.

The performance was assessed using the metrics described in Sect. 3.2. The MRE for each individual landmark (PS1, PS2, FH1) are reported, demonstrating detailed localization accuracy across different anatomical points. Additionally, we introduce average Mean Absolute Error (MAE) computed for the coordinates of three landmarks to provide a more comprehensive assessment of localization precision.

The method achieved a mean AoP error of 8.37° on the test set, with average landmark localization(disantce) accuracy of 21.83 pixels.

Computational Efficiency Analysis. While accuracy is a primary metric for clinical applications, computational efficiency is important for real-time assessment in clinical environments. We conducted a comprehensive analysis of computational resource utilization [22] during inference on the test set, providing valuable benchmarks for future lightweight model development efforts. These efficiency metrics, though not part of the challenge evaluation criteria, establish important baselines for subsequent optimization research.

The area under curve (AUC) metrics provide an integrated view of resource consumption over time, offering a more comprehensive assessment than peak values alone.

The resource utilization was monitored during model inference using the test set, capturing GPU memory usage, CPU utilization, and RAM consumption over time. Table 3 summarizes the key computational efficiency metrics.

Figure 2 visualizes the resource usage patterns during model inference. The time-series plots demonstrate the evolving computational demands throughout the inference process, with notable observations including a rapid increase in GPU memory allocation during model initialization, followed by stable utilization during inference, and progressive RAM consumption over time.

Table 3. Computational efficiency metrics for the baseline model.

Metric	Value
Runtime (s)	17.66
Maximum GPU Memory (MB)	6,694
GPU Memory-Time AUC (MB·s)	117,188
Maximum CPU Utilization (%)	19.32
CPU Utilization-Time AUC (%·s)	144.96
Maximum RAM Usage (MB)	37,831.25
RAM-Time AUC (MB·s)	644,770

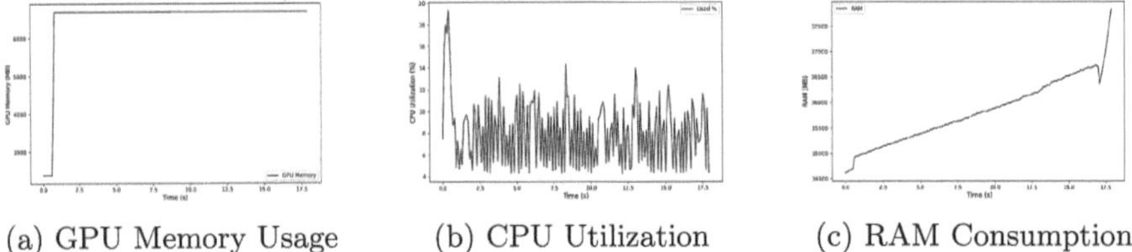

(a) GPU Memory Usage   (b) CPU Utilization   (c) RAM Consumption

Fig. 2. Time-series visualization of computational resource utilization during model inference.

Qualitative Analysis In addition to quantitative metrics, we generate visual overlays of predicted landmarks and heatmaps on test images to facilitate qualitative assessment. These visualizations enable expert evaluation of predicted landmark placements and identification of systematic errors.

In Fig. 3 ,we illustrate comparison of Ground Truth annotations (top row) and model predictions (bottom row) for ultrasound image feature point detec-

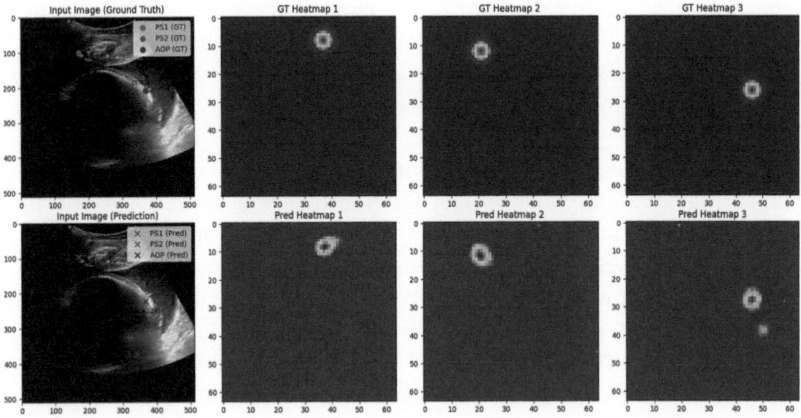

Fig. 3. Comparison of Ground Truth annotations and model predictions

tion. The Ground Truth group (left: ultrasound image and three heatmaps) marks red (PS1), green (PS2), and blue (FH1) dots; the Prediction group (left: ultrasound image and three heatmaps) indicates predicted points with "×" symbols in corresponding colors. Heatmaps transition from blue (low probability) to red/yellow (high probability), showing differences in localization confidence.

4   Discussion

The baseline method presented in this paper demonstrates the effectiveness of heatmap-based keypoint detection for AoP measurement. As a baseline approach, it has limitations that provide participants with room for improvement.

The main limitations of the baseline method include using only 300 annotated samples for training, employing a standard U-Net [23] architecture, implementing simple post-processing methods, and inadequate consideration of clinical anomalies.

Participants can explore improvement directions including: leveraging the large amount of unlabeled data through semi-supervised learning, adopting more advanced network architectures , integrating anatomical prior knowledge, and optimizing post-processing techniques.

Additionally, our computational efficiency analysis (runtime: 17.66s, GPU memory: 6,694MB, RAM: 37,831MB) suggests potential for optimization through techniques like pruning and quantization. Future work should explore lightweight architectures while maintaining clinical accuracy.

Technical challenges primarily include domain generalization capability, adaptation to anatomical variability, achieving real-time performance, and improving model explainability. We expect participants to focus not only on improving technical metrics but also on the clinical applicability and robustness of their solutions.

5   Conclusion

This study presents a baseline method for AoP measurement in intrapartum ultrasound images based on heatmap regression for keypoint detection. Despite using limited annotated data, the method achieves an average AoP error of 8.37° and a MRE of 21.83 pixels, demonstrating the feasibility of automated AoP measurement.

The IUGC2025 challenge aims to advance artificial intelligence technologies in obstetric ultrasound imaging, particularly through keypoint detection for more accurate and objective labor assessment. This baseline method provides participants with a starting point, showcasing both the potential and limitations of foundational approaches.

We encourage participants to explore innovative methodologies, leverage the large amount of unlabeled data, integrate clinical knowledge, and consider diverse clinical scenarios. Successful solutions will directly contribute to the advancement of obstetric clinical practice by providing more precise decision support tools, ultimately improving maternal and neonatal health outcomes.

Acknowledgements. This work was supported by the Natural Science Foundation of Guangdong Province (2023A1515012833 to J.B.; 2024A1515011886 to J.B), the National Natural Science Foundation of China (61901192 to J.B.), High-end Foreign Experts Recruitment Plan of China (H20240205 to J.B.), China Scholarship Council (202206785002 to J.B.) and the Guangdong Health Economics Association (2025-WJHX-17).

The authors have no competing interests to declare that are relevant to the content of this article.

References

1. Rosenberg, K.R., Trevathan, W.R.: Evolutionary perspectives on cesarean section. Evol. Med. Public Health **2018**(1), 67–81 (2018)

2. Gregory, K.D., Jackson, S., Korst, L., Fridman, M.: Cesarean versus vaginal delivery: whose risks? whose benefits? Am. J. Perinatol. **29**(01), 07–18 (2012)

3. Sandall, J., Tribe, R.M., Avery, L., Mola, G., Visser, G.H., Homer, C.S., Gibbons, D., Kelly, N.M., Kennedy, H.P., Kidanto, H., et al.: Short-term and long-term effects of caesarean section on the health of women and children. The Lancet **392**(10155), 1349–1357 (2018)

4. Seval, M.M., Yuce, T., Kalafat, E., Duman, B., Aker, S., Kumbasar, H., Koc, A.: Comparison of effects of digital vaginal examination with transperineal ultrasound during labor on pain and anxiety levels: a randomized controlled trial (2016)

5. Tutschek, B., Torkildsen, E., Eggebø, T.: Comparison between ultrasound parameters and clinical examination to assess fetal head station in labor. Ultrasound Obstet. Gynecol. **41**(4), 425–429 (2013)

6. Tutschek, B., Braun, T., Chantraine, F., Henrich, W.: A study of progress of labour using intrapartum translabial ultrasound, assessing head station, direction, and angle of descent. BJOG Int. J. Obstet. Gynaecol. **118**(1), 62–69 (2011)

7. Bellussi, F., Ghi, T., Youssef, A., Cataneo, I., Salsi, G., Simonazzi, G., Pilu, G.: Intrapartum ultrasound to differentiate flexion and deflexion in occipitoposterior rotation. Fetal Diagn. Ther. **42**(4), 249–256 (2017)

8. Malvasi, A., Tinelli, A., Barbera, A., Eggebø, T., Mynbaev, O., Bochicchio, M., Pacella, E., Di Renzo, G.: Occiput posterior position diagnosis: vaginal examination or intrapartum sonography? a clinical review. J. Matern. Fetal Neonatal Med. **27**(5), 520–526 (2014)

9. Youssef, A., Salsi, G., Montaguti, E., Bellussi, F., Pacella, G., Azzarone, C., Farina, A., Rizzo, N., Pilu, G.: Automated measurement of the angle of progression in labor: a feasibility and reliability study. Fetal Diagn. Ther. **41**(4), 293–299 (2017)

10. Youssef, A., Brunelli, E., Azzarone, C., Di Donna, G., Casadio, P., Pilu, G.: Fetal head progression and regression on maternal pushing at term and labor outcome. Ultrasound Obstet. Gynecol. **58**(1), 105–110 (2021)

11. Ghi, T., Eggebø, T., Lees, C., Kalache, K., Rozenberg, P., Youssef, A., Salomon, L., Tutschek, B.: Isuog practice guidelines: intrapartum ultrasound. Ultrasound Obstet. Gynecol. **52**(1), 128–139 (2018)

12. Lu, Y., Zhou, M., Zhi, D., Zhou, M., Jiang, X., Qiu, R., Ou, Z., Wang, H., Qiu, D., Zhong, M., et al.: The JNU-IFM dataset for segmenting pubic symphysis-fetal head. Data Brief **41**, 107904 (2022)

13. Rueda, S., Fathima, S., Knight, C.L., Yaqub, M., Papageorghiou, A.T., Rahmatullah, B., Foi, A., Maggioni, M., Pepe, A., Tohka, J., et al.: Evaluation and comparison of current fetal ultrasound image segmentation methods for biometric measurements: a grand challenge. IEEE Trans. Med. Imaging **33**(4), 797–813 (2013)
14. Dietz, H.P.: Ultrasound imaging of the pelvic floor part i: two-dimensional aspects. Ultrasound Obstet. Gynecol. **23**(1), 80–92 (2004)
15. Chen, Z., Ou, Z., Lu, Y., Bai, J.: Direction-guided and multi-scale feature screening for fetal head-pubic symphysis segmentation and angle of progression calculation. Expert Syst. Appl. **245**, 123096 (2024)
16. Chen, Z., Lu, Y., Long, S., Campello, V.M., Bai, J., Lekadir, K.: Fetal head and pubic symphysis segmentation in intrapartum ultrasound image using a dual-path boundary-guided residual network. IEEE J. Biomed. Health Inform. **28**(8), 4648–4659 (2024)
17. Zhou, M., Yuan, C., Chen, Z., Wang, C., Lu, Y.: Automatic angle of progress measurement of intrapartum transperineal ultrasound image with deep learning. In: Martel, A.L., Abolmaesumi, P., Stoyanov, D., Mateus, D., Zuluaga, M.A., Zhou, S.K., Racoceanu, D., Joskowicz, L. (eds.) Medical Image Computing and Computer Assisted Intervention—MICCAI 2020, pp. 406–414. Springer International Publishing, Cham (2020)
18. Lu, Y., Zhi, D., Zhou, M., Lai, F., Chen, G., Ou, Z., Zeng, R., Long, S., Qiu, R., Zhou, M., Jiang, X., Wang, H., Bai, J.: Multitask deep neural network for the fully automatic measurement of the angle of progression. Comput. Math. Methods Med. **2022**(1), 5192338 (2022)
19. Zhou, Z., Lu, Y., Bai, J., Campello, V.M., Feng, F., Lekadir, K.: Segment anything model for fetal head-pubic symphysis segmentation in intrapartum ultrasound image analysis. Expert Syst. Appl. **263**, 125699 (2025)
20. Thaler, F., Payer, C., Urschler, M., Stern, D.: Modeling annotation uncertainty with gaussian heatmaps in landmark localization. arXiv preprint arXiv:2109.09533 (2021)
21. Marmolin, H.: Subjective MSE measures. IEEE Trans. Syst. Man Cybern. **16**(3), 486–489 (1986)
22. Ma, J., Zhang, Y., Gu, S.: Fast and low-GPU-memory abdomen CT organ segmentation: the flare challenge. Med. Image Anal. **82**, 102616 (2022)
23. Ronneberger, O., Fischer, P., Brox, T.: U-net: convolutional networks for biomedical image segmentation. In: Medical Image Computing and Computer-Assisted Intervention–MICCAI 2015: 18th International Conference, Munich, Germany, 5–9 October 2015, Proceedings, part III, vol. 18, pp. 234–241. Springer (2015)

J. Bai et al. (Eds.): IUGC 2025, LNCS 16317, pp. 119–120, 2026.
https://doi.org/10.1007/978-3-032-11616-1